Scary Ancient Egypt History Facts

CRAFTED BY SKRIUWER

Copyright © 2025 by Skriuwer.

All rights reserved. No part of this book may be used or reproduced in any form whatsoever without written permission except in the case of brief quotations in critical articles or reviews.

At **Skriuwer**, we're more than just a team—we're a global community of people who love books. In Frisian, "Skriuwer" means "writer," and that's at the heart of what we do: creating and sharing books with readers worldwide. Wherever you are in the world, **Skriuwer** is here to inspire learning.

Frisian is one of the oldest languages in Europe, closely related to English and Dutch, and is spoken by about **500,000 people** in the province of **Friesland** (Fryslân), located in the northern Netherlands. It's the second official language of the Netherlands, but like many minority languages, Frisian faces the challenge of survival in a modern, globalized world.

We're using the money we earn to promote the Frisian language.

For more information, contact : **kontakt@skriuwer.com** (www.skriuwer.com)

Disclaimer:
The images in this book are creative reinterpretations of historical scenes. While every effort was made to accurately capture the essence of the periods depicted, some illustrations may include artistic embellishments or approximations. They are intended to evoke the atmosphere and spirit of the times rather than serve as precise historical records.

TABLE OF CONTENTS

CHAPTER 1: INTRODUCTION TO ANCIENT EGYPT AND THE NILE

- Landscape of Egypt and the importance of the Nile's floods
- Early settlement patterns and lurking dangers
- The role of fear in shaping basic social and religious ideas

CHAPTER 2: PREDYNASTIC EGYPT AND THE RISE OF KINGS

- Small communities evolving into early kingdoms
- Human sacrifice possibilities and early religious beliefs
- Foundations for dynastic rule and fear-based power

CHAPTER 3: EARLY DYNASTIES AND THE FIRST HORRORS IN BURIAL CUSTOMS

- Formation of a unified throne and the concept of divine kingship
- Evidence of retainer sacrifice in royal tombs
- Emergence of curses and extreme measures to protect burials

CHAPTER 4: STEP PYRAMIDS, HUMAN SACRIFICES, AND THE AFTERLIFE

- King Djoser's monumental Step Pyramid at Saqqara
- Rumors of human sacrifices to serve the dead king
- Increasing complexity in afterlife beliefs and potential tomb traps

CHAPTER 5: OLD KINGDOM MONUMENTS AND THE FRIGHTENING SIDE OF PYRAMID BUILDING

- Massive labor forces under pharaohs like Sneferu and Khufu
- Harsh punishments, forced labor, and rumored curses
- Society's dependence on fear-based control

CHAPTER 6: FIRST INTERMEDIATE PERIOD: CHAOS AND FEAR

- Collapse of central authority and widespread famine
- Rise of local warlords and brutal reprisals
- Tomb robberies, temple desecration, and social breakdown

CHAPTER 7: MIDDLE KINGDOM – TOMB ROBBERIES AND DARK RITUALS

- Reunification under new pharaohs yet continued fear of afterlife threats
- Proliferation of more refined funerary customs and protective spells
- Tomb robbing and black magic persisting beneath apparent stability

CHAPTER 8: MILITARY MIGHT IN THE MIDDLE KINGDOM AND THE HORRORS OF WARFARE

- Expansion into Nubia and clashes with neighboring regions
- Conscripted armies, brutal conquests, and public terror
- Use of fear-based diplomacy and the psychological impact of battles

CHAPTER 9: THE NEW KINGDOM'S VALLEY OF THE KINGS AND TOMB CURSES

- *Hidden royal burials aimed at thwarting tomb robbers*
- *Mythic curses, demon-guardians, and labyrinthine passages*
- *Artisans' secrecy and the aura of dread surrounding the valley*

CHAPTER 10: THE CULT OF AMUN AND TERRIFYING RELIGIOUS POWER

- *Amun's dominance and priests' growing influence*
- *Oracles that could condemn individuals without appeal*
- *Tension between pharaohs and a priesthood wielding fear as a tool*

CHAPTER 11: THE REIGN OF HATSHEPSUT AND UNKNOWN THREATS

- *A female pharaoh's struggle for legitimacy amid hidden conspiracies*
- *Mortuary temple at Deir el-Bahri and clandestine temple activities*
- *Court intrigues, suppressed rumors, and the careful balance of power*

CHAPTER 12: AKHENATEN'S RELIGIOUS SHIFT AND DREAD AMONG THE MASSES

- *Radical monotheism targeting old gods and temples*
- *Cultural shock, social chaos, and fear of divine retaliation*
- *Abandonment of tradition and the possibility of cosmic ruin*

CHAPTER 13: TUTANKHAMUN'S TOMB – HIDDEN DANGERS AND GHOSTLY LEGENDS

- A boy-king's hurried burial and rumor-fueled curses
- Claustrophobic tomb chambers brimming with valuables
- Tales of restless spirits, early tomb robbers, and fearful guardians

CHAPTER 14: THE RAMESES ERA – CLASH OF EMPIRES AND HORRORS OF WAR

- Massive militarization under Seti I and Rameses II
- Brutal campaigns, forced labor, and terrifying battlefield scenes
- Empire-building through intimidation and persistent human cost

CHAPTER 15: THE LATE PERIOD – INVASIONS, DESTRUCTIONS, AND DARK OMENS

- Nubian, Assyrian, and Persian conquests ravaging the Nile Valley
- Foreign occupiers looting temples and subjugating cities
- Ominous prophecies, chaotic rebellions, and the gods' fading presence

CHAPTER 16: MAGIC AND SORCERY – REALMS OF FEAR IN ANCIENT EGYPT

- Daily reliance on spells for healing yet dread of dark magic
- Secret texts and forbidden rites overshadowed by suspicion
- Exorcisms, demon encounters, and the double-edged nature of sorcery

CHAPTER 17: DEMONS, SPIRITS, AND THE AFTERLIFE'S MONSTERS

- Malevolent spirits prowling deserts and haunted corners of cities
- Monstrous gatekeepers in the underworld and the terror of Apophis
- Eternal threat of demonic attacks fueling elaborate protective beliefs

---

CHAPTER 18: GRAVE GOODS AND MACABRE BURIAL PRACTICES

- Overflow of tomb furnishings, retainer sacrifices in early eras
- Grisly embalming processes, canopic jars, and bizarre funerary art
- Nightmarish tomb traps, lingering curses, and the unsettling army of shabtis

---

CHAPTER 19: ANCIENT EGYPTIAN MEDICINE, CURSES, AND SUPERSTITIONS

- Healing as a fight against demonic forces and malignant spells
- Frightening concoctions, excrement-based remedies, and curses for hire
- Birthing rituals, "evil eye," and the pervasive unease shaping medical beliefs

---

CHAPTER 20: DECLINE OF ANCIENT EGYPT AND ECHOES OF FEAR

- Slow fragmentation under foreign invasions and eroding priesthoods
- Cultural identity overshadowed by Greek, Persian, and Roman domination
- Tomb lootings, lost scripts, and the final lingering dread as pharaonic power waned

CHAPTER 1

Introduction to Ancient Egypt and the Nile

Ancient Egypt rose along the banks of the Nile River in North Africa. The land of Egypt is often seen as a narrow strip of green on both sides of this mighty river, surrounded by vast deserts. The Nile shaped everything about Egyptian life—the food they ate, the crops they grew, the houses they built, the gods they prayed to, and even their fears. In this first chapter, we will explore the geography and early settlement patterns in Ancient Egypt and learn about the scary aspects that might have haunted these early settlers. We will also look at how nature itself, including the floods and the desert, could be both a blessing and a curse.

1.1 The Nile: Lifeline and Threat

The Nile was the source of life in Egypt. It provided water for drinking and farming in an otherwise dry area. Every year, the river would flood, depositing a thick layer of fertile silt on its banks. After the floodwaters drained, the land near the river became perfect for growing wheat, barley, and other crops. This predictable cycle gave the Egyptians enough food to feed a growing population.

But the Nile could also bring disaster. Sometimes, the floods were too high. Villages would be destroyed, and fields wiped out. Other times, the river barely rose at all. Crop failures caused starvation, which led to disease and unrest. People were frightened when the usual cycle was disrupted, believing the gods might be angry.

Even crocodiles in the river posed a danger. They lurked beneath the waters, waiting to attack unsuspecting humans. Hippopotamuses were also a threat, known to overturn boats and crush people. These terrifying creatures were feared and respected. Ancient Egyptians sometimes worshipped gods with crocodile heads (like Sobek) because they believed honoring these animals might protect them.

1.2 Early Settlements: Clusters of Huts in the Shadows of the Desert

Long before pyramids and grand temples, simple huts made of reeds or mud brick were scattered near the Nile. These early communities formed because people needed to be close to the water for survival. The desert was unforgiving, with scorching days and freezing nights. Sandstorms could arrive suddenly, scratching skin and filling lungs with dust.

The boundary between the fertile land (called the "Black Land" because of the dark silt) and the desert (called the "Red Land") was very clear. The desert was frightening to many early Egyptians. If someone wandered too far without enough water, they could die of thirst. Bandits or nomadic raiders might hide among the dunes, ready to attack a poorly guarded settlement. People told stories around fires at night of lost travelers stumbling upon hidden tombs or monstrous desert creatures. These early tales helped shape the Egyptian imagination about the afterlife and dangerous spirits lurking beyond the safety of the Nile.

1.3 Beginnings of Religious Belief: Fear of the Unknown

As early Egyptians tried to explain the forces around them—floods, droughts, death—they developed spiritual ideas. They believed that many gods controlled the universe. Because nature could be cruel, some of these gods had frightening qualities. They might demand offerings and respect to keep disasters away.

One of the earliest known deities was a form of a mother goddess figure who was both nurturing and punishing. Storms, diseases, and snake bites were often explained as signs that the gods were angry. People would leave small figurines, food, or even animal sacrifices near important spots by the river or in the desert, hoping to appease these spirits. The fear of not pleasing the gods ran deep.

Over time, these beliefs led to the concept that certain people—shamans, priests, or wise men—could communicate with the gods. This created a power system where religious leaders held a grip over people by telling them how to avoid the gods' wrath. It laid the foundation for later pharaohs, who claimed they were chosen by the divine.

1.4 The Dangerous Path to Civilization: Conflict and Control

As small villages grew, conflicts began over resources like water, farmland, and trade routes. Some leaders gained influence by being skilled warriors or having close ties with religious figures. Their followers believed these leaders could protect them from enemies and curses. But the leaders also used fear to control the people. They might threaten to punish or exile those who did not follow their rules.

Evidence of skirmishes can be found in ancient burial sites. Archaeologists have discovered skeletons bearing signs of violent death—broken skulls, arrow injuries, and other wounds. This suggests that the struggle for land and power was brutal. Early Egyptians also believed that the spirits of those who died violently might wander the earth, seeking revenge if not properly buried. This idea of restless ghosts added another layer of fear to everyday life.

1.5 The Nile and Early Magic: Trying to Tame Nature

The cycle of flooding was mostly predictable, but not always. When it went wrong, entire communities could starve. Early Egyptians turned to magic and rituals to ensure the right balance of water. They created charms, amulets, and performed ceremonies to please the Nile gods. Some of these rites might have included animal sacrifices, chanting in small groups, and burying offerings in the riverbank. These ceremonies were secretive and sometimes frightening. People believed that if a single person performed a ritual incorrectly, it could anger the gods, bringing doom upon everyone.

Magic in Egypt became complex over time. Early forms were simpler but still based on the idea that the supernatural world was near and had to be controlled. Charms might be shaped like small crocodiles to ward off real crocodiles. Clay dolls or figurines might be used to represent enemies. Destroying these figures in a ritual setting was thought to weaken or kill the enemies in real life. This practice would evolve in later centuries into more detailed spells inscribed on papyrus or temple walls.

1.6 Desert Dangers: Scorpions and Serpents

The desert around the Nile was not empty. It was teeming with dangerous creatures like scorpions and venomous snakes. Bites and stings often led to slow, painful deaths, especially when there was no medical help. This constant threat gave rise to gods and goddesses linked to protection from venomous animals. One such deity was Selket (also spelled Serqet), often shown with a scorpion on her head.

Stories of how people died from these animals spread quickly, creating a fear that lurked in the background of daily life. Parents warned children not to wander too far from the settlement at dusk or dawn when scorpions might come out in the open. This fear eventually became part of the culture's spiritual beliefs, weaving into medical texts that included magical spells meant to treat bites.

1.7 Trade and Encounters with Strangers: Fear of the Unknown

As early communities in Egypt expanded, some people began traveling or trading goods like grain, pottery, and stone tools with neighboring regions. Contact with people from across the deserts or from lands south of the Nile introduced new items, but also new fears. Strangers were sometimes seen as threats who brought unfamiliar gods and diseases.

Conflict between trade partners could lead to armed skirmishes. Military power at this stage was basic—spears, clubs, and simple bows—but it was deadly enough to instill terror. Raiding parties might sneak into a village at night, setting huts on fire and stealing food and livestock. Survivors would tell grim stories for generations. Some artifacts found in desert outposts, such as battered skulls or broken weapons, hint at these violent encounters.

1.8 Ritual Burials: Seeds of a Dark Tradition

Even in these very early times, Egyptians were careful about burying their dead. They often chose high ground where floods could not disturb graves. Bodies were sometimes buried with pots of food, tools, or personal items. They believed the dead might need these things in another world. But if a person died tragically or with unresolved anger, that spirit could haunt the living.

To prevent hauntings, certain rites would be performed by the relatives. If these rites were not done properly, people feared the spirit would wander, causing crops to fail or sickness to spread. Early grave goods sometimes included a small figurine of a servant, meant to carry out tasks for the dead in the afterlife. Over time, these practices would become more complex and more frightening in their details.

1.9 The Grim Reality of Everyday Life

Life in ancient Egypt, even in the earliest phases, was not just about building or farming. Disease was widespread, and medical knowledge was limited. People lived with constant risks—wild animals, sickness, violence, and the unpredictability of nature. Because of these dangers, religion and superstition became a major part of day-to-day living.

Frightening stories were told to keep children and adults away from risky behaviors. Rumors of shape-shifting demons in the desert or curses carried on the wind reinforced the idea that safety lay in community, not in isolation. Although some of these stories may have been exaggerated, they served the purpose of cautioning people about real dangers and encouraging them to respect the power of the unseen world.

1.10 The Role of Fear in Shaping Early Society

Fear was a strong force that helped shape the rules of early Egyptian society. Leaders used fear of the gods, fear of curses, and fear of the unknown to keep order. People believed that if they did not obey their leaders, they would lose divine favor. They also believed that curses could be used against them if they broke sacred laws.

Some villages might have practiced harsh punishments for crimes, such as cutting off a thief's hand or forcing someone into the desert without supplies. The message was clear: step out of line, and you risked both human and supernatural wrath. This fear-based control set a precedent for later dynasties, where the pharaoh was seen as a living god on earth.

1.11 Early Art and Its Haunting Imagery

Archaeologists have found pottery and small sculptures from Predynastic times with strange, sometimes disturbing images. Figures with raised arms, possibly representing dancing or worship, but also possibly representing aggression or magical rites. Some vases show groups of bound captives, suggesting warfare or ritual sacrifice.

Symbols like the falcon, which would later be associated with Horus, appear in early art. Horus became a god representing sky, kingship, and protection, but even these protective symbols had a scary side. The falcon could be fierce and deadly when hunting. Early Egyptians watched hawks and vultures tear apart prey, reminding them of the harsh realities of life and death.

1.12 Toward the Rise of Kings

By the end of what we call Predynastic times, the idea of powerful rulers was forming. Some leaders managed to unify small territories under their command. They might have used fearsome displays, such as the heads of defeated enemies on stakes, to show their authority. Tombs for these leaders became more elaborate, reflecting the belief that their power continued after death.

This chapter has shown how ancient Egyptians lived in a land that was both generous and cruel. The Nile gave them food but could also destroy. The desert protected them from invaders but held deadly creatures. Life was a delicate balance, full of unknowns. Fear and respect for the gods, spirits, and nature guided them. This set the stage for the rise of kings who would later claim divine status to rule their people. Yet with great power also came great fear, as the next chapters will reveal.

CHAPTER 2

Predynastic Egypt and the Rise of Kings

In this chapter, we will explore the time before Egypt was officially unified under a single pharaoh—often referred to as the Predynastic period. During this era, people developed many of the customs and beliefs that would shape Egyptian civilization for thousands of years. These included early forms of worship, burial practices, and the use of fear as a means of social control. We will look at how kingship emerged from local chieftains, how symbols of power and terror appeared in artifacts, and how the seeds of larger dynasties were planted in these formative times.

2.1 Defining the Predynastic Period

Historians typically define the Predynastic period as beginning around 5000 BCE and ending around 3100 BCE when the first true dynastic ruling line was formed under a single king (often referred to as Narmer or Menes). Though these dates vary slightly among scholars, what is certain is that this was a time of change and experimentation in Egypt.

During the Predynastic period, communities grew along the Nile, trading with each other and sometimes fighting for resources. Early forms of writing, such as pictorial signs, began to emerge, though they were not yet the fully developed hieroglyphs we associate with later periods.

What made this era frightening for many was the lack of centralized authority. Different regions had different customs. Some leaders seemed keen on showing their might in gruesome ways—by executing captured enemies or leaving them to the desert beasts. Without a single set of laws, chaos was never far away.

2.2 Local Chieftains and War

Predynastic Egypt was divided into small territories we often call nomes. Each nome had its own leader or chieftain. Some were more aggressive and tried to expand their control. Warfare was a regular part of life, and fear of raids or invasions was common. Settlements close to the deserts were especially vulnerable to attacks by nomads.

Archaeological sites reveal mass graves with signs of violent death—spears, arrows, or blunt force trauma. Scholars suggest these could be evidence of conflicts between rival nomes. While the idea of large-scale warfare like in later dynasties may not be accurate for this early stage, regional skirmishes were enough to make life uncertain. Leaders who promised protection, even if they used brutal methods, could gain followers. Fear helped them maintain power.

2.3 The Emergence of Social Classes

As some chieftains gained wealth, they built stronger houses, had more luxurious items, and commissioned better graves for themselves and their families. Common people lived in simpler homes and were buried in basic pits. This disparity created social classes. With inequality came fear: fear of angering the powerful, fear of losing one's property or being enslaved, and fear of not having proper rites performed after death.

Those who rebelled or failed to show loyalty might be cast out or worse. At the same time, loyalty to a strong leader might grant protection from outside threats. This balance of power and submission grew stronger as chieftains became kings.

2.4 Early Religious Practices

Religion in Predynastic Egypt was closely linked to nature. The Nile, the sun, and animals like bulls or crocodiles became important symbols. Temples as we know them did not exist yet, but there were sacred spots, possibly marked with stones or wooden posts, where people left offerings. Animal bones, broken pottery, and charred remains point to rituals that might have included small-scale sacrifices.

One particularly frightening aspect was the use of human remains in ceremonies. While evidence is limited, some archaeologists believe certain rituals might have involved burying victims with a leader. Skulls of decapitated individuals found near elite graves lead to speculation of human sacrifice or retainer sacrifice, where servants were killed to continue serving the leader in the afterlife.

2.5 Mysterious Animal Cults

In later Egyptian history, we see fully developed animal cults worshipping gods like Bastet (the cat goddess) and Apis (the bull). The roots of these practices can be traced back to Predynastic times. Early rock carvings show cows, bulls, and other animals in what seems like ritual contexts. Since animals were vital for food, transport, and farming, worshipping them or using them as symbols of power was natural.

But these early animal cults could also be violent. Some chieftains might have showcased bull heads on poles at city entrances. The bull, known for its strength and aggression, became a symbol of both fertility and destruction. The threat was clear: an invading force would face the same fate as the sacrificial bull if they dared to attack.

2.6 Artifacts of Fear and Power

One of the best-known artifacts from the Predynastic period is the Narmer Palette, which dates to around 3100 BCE. It is a ceremonial stone palette that depicts King Narmer, who is often credited with unifying Upper and Lower Egypt. The scenes show Narmer striking down enemies, and there are rows of decapitated bodies. This suggests that fear and violence were central to the king's image of authority.

Though the Narmer Palette marks the transition from Predynastic to Dynastic Egypt, its style has roots in earlier artifacts. Predynastic pots and palettes often depicted conflict, wild animals, and symbols of control. The repeated motifs of bound captives and triumphant leaders reveal a culture where power was flaunted through images of subjugation and bloodshed.

2.7 Early Writing and Its Dark Messages

Before full hieroglyphs, there were simpler pictorial signs. Some carvings show ominous symbols like severed heads or rows of bound captives. While we cannot fully decipher all these early markings, it seems likely they served as warnings or records of successful raids.

As writing evolved, it became a tool to spread both religion and fear. A leader's name or symbol carved on a boundary might claim ownership of the land. Anyone who crossed that boundary could face supernatural punishment, as well as real violence from the local warriors. Even at this early stage, writing had the power to intimidate and control.

2.8 Death Rites and the Seeds of Mummification

In Predynastic times, bodies were often buried in shallow graves. The hot, dry sand naturally preserved some remains, leaving them desiccated or mummified. This accidental preservation sparked ideas that a well-preserved body might be important for the afterlife. Over time, the Egyptians came to see dryness and preservation as a path to eternal life.

What began as a natural occurrence would develop into a complex ritual in later centuries, with removal of organs and special embalming. But even at this early stage, the concept of preserving the body to avoid decay—and potentially to avoid angry ghosts—was taking shape. People feared that if a spirit's body was left to rot or be eaten by animals, that spirit might wander and torment the living.

2.9 Human Sacrifice: Myth or Reality?

One of the most debated topics among Egyptologists is the extent of human sacrifice in Predynastic and early Dynastic Egypt. Some archaeologists argue that tombs of elite individuals contain secondary burials of people who might have been killed to serve the leader in the afterlife. Others believe these may be voluntary retainers or unrelated burials placed close by as an act of respect.

Despite the debate, enough evidence suggests that some form of retainer sacrifice or forced killing could have happened. The idea that an important leader would take his servants, guards, or even wives with him to the grave was a terrifying prospect. Whether or not it was widespread, the possibility of such practices added to the aura of fear surrounding royal burials.

2.10 Growth of Urban Centers and the Temple's Role

Toward the end of the Predynastic period, towns in Upper and Lower Egypt grew bigger, including places like Hierakonpolis, Naqada, and Buto. At Hierakonpolis, for example, archaeologists found large ceremonial complexes, suggesting advanced religious practices. Shrines or early temples might have hosted rituals not open to the public. Animal bones, beer jars, and other offerings indicate feasting and possibly sacrificial rites.

Priests or religious leaders gained influence by claiming knowledge of how to communicate with gods or spirits. This often involved chanting, drumming, or the use of hallucinogenic substances. The secrecy of these rituals frightened common people, who believed that crossing a priest might lead to curses or divine punishment.

2.11 Early Pharaohs and Divine Authority

As the Predynastic period neared its end, powerful chieftains began to take on divine titles. They claimed they were sons of gods or incarnations of gods on earth. This belief set the stage for the pharaohs of later periods. With divine authority came the power to demand obedience. The populace was taught that disobeying the ruler was the same as disobeying the gods.

Stories circulated of kings who unleashed plagues, floods, or swarms of pests on those who refused tribute. Even if these tales were exaggerated, they kept people in line. Fear was one of the tools these early rulers used to weld together the separate regions of Egypt under a single throne.

2.12 Warfare Technology Advances

Though still in its infancy, military technology was improving by the late Predynastic period. Better flint knives, maces, and bows meant more effective killing. Warriors trained to fight in formations, and alliances formed between nomes to defeat mutual enemies. The image of a king with a mace smiting enemies became a common artistic theme.

These developments created a culture where violence was normalized. Towns needed fortifications. Armies carried out pre-emptive strikes. And behind it all was the widespread belief that the gods approved of victorious warriors. This approval was essential for a ruler who wanted to prove his might. It was not just about winning battles, but about showing the entire population that the gods stood behind him.

2.13 Signs of Unification and the Final Push

As we approach 3100 BCE, leaders like Narmer appear in the archaeological record. The Narmer Palette, along with other artifacts, show the conquest of Lower Egypt by a ruler from Upper Egypt. Whether this was a single decisive battle or a series of smaller campaigns is unknown. What is clear is that Narmer adopted symbols from both regions, including the crowns of Upper and Lower Egypt, to present himself as a unifying figure.

Fear played a significant role in this unification process. Depictions of rows of decapitated enemies made it clear what would happen to those who resisted. Regions that submitted were spared, but likely paid heavy tribute. This pattern of conquest, followed by harsh punishment for rebels, would become a hallmark of later dynasties as well.

2.14 Transformation into the Early Dynastic Period

By the end of the Predynastic period, Egypt was on the brink of becoming a nation with a single leader. Many historians see this as the start of the Early Dynastic period (around 3100–2686 BCE). The scary aspects from Predynastic times—like fear-based rule, brutal rituals, and constant conflict—did not go away. Instead, they were embedded into the new kingdom's culture.

The divine kingship model made the ruler not just a political figure, but a living god. This gave him absolute power over life and death. Rituals became more organized, and burial practices grew in complexity. The seeds of pyramid building and sophisticated mummification would be planted in the upcoming centuries, building on the foundation laid in the Predynastic era.

CHAPTER 3

Early Dynasties and the First Horrors in Burial Customs

From around 3100 BCE, Egypt witnessed the rise of its first dynasties—often called the Early Dynastic Period. This era marks the time when the scattered communities across the Nile Valley formally united under a succession of kings. These rulers, who would later be called "pharaohs," expanded their power over Upper and Lower Egypt. Their authority rested on more than just military might; they also laid the groundwork for state-sponsored religion, a formidable bureaucracy, and deeply unsettling burial customs that many find haunting even now. In this chapter, we will take a close look at the Early Dynastic rulers, the expansion of fearful beliefs tied to kingship, and the new ways the dead were treated—ways that might have made a common Egyptian tremble in awe or dread.

3.1 Birth of a Unified Throne

When King Narmer (often identified with Menes by later traditions) came to power, Egypt was divided into two lands: Upper Egypt in the south and Lower Egypt in the north. Thanks to military campaigns and political alliances, Narmer and his successors managed to bring these lands together under one crown. This unification process did not happen peacefully. According to ancient carvings, the losers in battle sometimes faced horrific punishments, including decapitation and the display of severed heads on poles. Such cruelty served a purpose: it terrorized any rebels or local chieftains who considered resisting the new king's authority.

Several kings followed Narmer, ruling from about 3100 BCE to 2686 BCE. This stretch of history is often grouped into the First and Second Dynasties. During these reigns, the concept of a single, divine king started to become normal throughout the Nile Valley. The king was not merely a warrior or a statesman—he was believed to be chosen by the gods, or even part god himself. This aura of sanctity gave him the right to command absolute loyalty. Anyone who defied the ruler risked severe physical punishment and spiritual doom.

3.2 Royal Cemeteries at Abydos and Saqqara

One of the most crucial developments during the Early Dynastic Period was the establishment of royal burial grounds. Two main sites rose to prominence: **Abydos** in Upper Egypt and **Saqqara** near the capital city of Memphis. At Abydos, a series of underground tombs formed the final resting place for early kings such as Djer, Djet, and others from the First Dynasty. Each tomb was marked on the surface by a simple structure, sometimes made of mud brick, that served as a memorial.

The tombs at Abydos and Saqqara reveal many unsettling features. Archaeologists have found what appear to be rows of subsidiary graves around the main royal tombs. Some experts believe these graves might hold the remains of servants or officials who were buried at the same time as the king—possibly sacrificed so they could serve him in the afterlife. This practice, if true, would indicate that human lives were taken to provide eternal companionship and labor for the deceased ruler. Even if these burials were not forced sacrifices, they still point to a culture that saw no problem in burying multiple individuals at once to form part of a king's funerary complex.

3.3 The Enclosure of the Dead King

Early Dynastic rulers were interred in large rectangular structures made of mud bricks, known later as "mastabas" (though the word mastaba is more often applied to slightly later, Old Kingdom tombs). These massive graves had multiple chambers, storage rooms, and offerings of food, pottery, and precious materials. The reason for such elaborate construction was rooted in the king's divine status. Egyptians believed that after death, the king became even more powerful, joining the realm of gods. To ensure he did not lack anything in the afterlife, they filled his tomb with an array of objects. Many of these items might seem harmless—like jars of beer, loaves of bread, or personal ornaments. But some large complexes also included weapons, imported luxury goods, and possibly even the bodies of sacrificed animals or people.

The enclosures surrounding these tombs were often high-walled and possibly guarded by soldiers. Some enclosures, like the one built for King Khasekhemwy, contained chapels or small shrines. When a king died, priests performed rituals that invoked protective deities to guard the royal remains. Anyone daring to break into these areas risked not just an earthly punishment—capture, torture, or death—but also spiritual retribution. Royal tomb inscriptions sometimes hinted that invaders or desecrators would be cursed forever. While direct textual curses from this time are rare, the symbolism in the tomb goods and artwork strongly suggests that fear played a role in deterring grave robbers.

3.4 Evidence of Human Sacrifice

One of the most debated topics in Early Dynastic studies is the possibility of **human sacrifice** at royal burials. Multiple tombs at Abydos dating to the First Dynasty show clusters of burials of young men and women. Their skeletons are well-preserved and often appear physically healthy, suggesting they died suddenly rather than from disease or old age. Furthermore, the arrangement of graves around the king's tomb hints these individuals were interred at the same time as their ruler.

Some archaeologists believe these were **retainer sacrifices**—that is, servants, soldiers, or household members who were put to death to serve their king in the afterlife. Others argue these people may have died in a plague or during a famine, their burials merely coinciding with the king's funeral. But given the patterns and the consistent age ranges of these "subsidiary" burials, the human sacrifice interpretation has gained traction among many scholars. If true, it shows a terrifying aspect of Early Dynastic rule: the king's passage to the afterlife might demand the forced death of his attendants.

3.5 The Use of Ritual Violence

Ritual violence was not limited to large-scale events like a king's funeral. The Early Dynastic Period also saw many smaller but significant displays of power. Some tombs and temples include depictions of the king striking enemies with a mace or smiting captives. These images were not merely for show; they conveyed the message that the king could—and would—violently crush anyone who opposed him. People living under this authority likely feared punishment not just in the mortal world, but in the afterlife if they failed to pay tribute or show devotion to the royal institution.

Punishments for crimes could be harsh. While detailed legal codes from this era are limited, evidence from later periods suggests that thieves could have limbs cut off, or they could be stoned to death. During the Early Dynastic Period, when central authority was still solidifying, the king or local governor might have resorted to extreme punishments to keep order. Tomb reliefs showcasing bound prisoners with tortured expressions underscore the reality that terror was a tool for governance.

3.6 Djer, Djet, and Other Early Dynastic Kings

Among the early kings was **Djer**, thought to be the second or third ruler of the First Dynasty. Little is known about his reign in terms of day-to-day governance, but he was buried at Abydos in a large tomb. Archaeological evidence from the site includes hundreds of small ivory labels depicting tributes and goods. These labels might have been attached to offerings. They also provide clues about trade networks and the variety of items used in funerary ceremonies.

Djet, another First Dynasty king, left behind a tomb stela depicting a snake-like form of the royal name. The stela's art suggests an emphasis on the king's protective and possibly threatening presence. People believed the king could transform into different forms, including dangerous creatures that symbolized both destruction and defense of sacred order.

3.7 The Horrifying Significance of Subsidiary Burials

For commoners, the idea that a king's death could demand the sacrifice of dozens—perhaps even hundreds—of individuals must have been terrifying. It signaled that the king, in his divine status, had the right to command not just wealth, but also the lives of his subjects. This system underscores an unsettling relationship between the living and the dead in Early Dynastic Egypt. To maintain the cosmos in balance, the king's tomb needed to be complete. If that included the presence of human attendants, so be it. Even if the practice was not universal or consistent across every reign, the knowledge that it could happen made the funeral of a king a solemn, awe-inspiring, and fearful event.

Interestingly, by the Second Dynasty, retainer sacrifice seems to have stopped or greatly diminished. Scholars debate the reason—perhaps the social system changed, and the practice became unpopular or politically risky. Another theory suggests that Egyptians shifted to using symbolic means (such as wooden servant statues, later known as shabtis) instead of actual human lives. Regardless of why it ended, its existence in the early dynasties remains one of the most unsettling aspects of Ancient Egyptian history.

3.8 The Royal Ideology of Terror and Protection

For the Egyptians, the king was a figure of contradictions. He offered protection from chaos, but he also inspired fear among his own people. Part of his role was to battle the forces of disorder (often personified as foreign enemies or mythic beasts) and uphold Maat, the principle of cosmic balance. This meant that when the king punished a wrongdoer or executed a captive, he was not just acting out of cruelty—he was carrying out a sacred duty to maintain order in the world. Such logic reinforced the bond between state violence and religious belief, making it hard for ordinary people to question or resist.

Even in everyday life, peasants might see the king's agents collecting taxes or conscripting men for labor. Anyone who refused could face severe penalties, including physical harm. The fear of punishment and the spiritual weight of opposing a divine king worked together to keep the population in check. The earliest temples dedicated to the king's cult, small though they were, reinforced the idea that the ruler deserved worship in life and after death. This gave religious backing to the entire structure of society.

3.9 Early Mastabas for Nobles and Officials

It was not only kings who had special tombs. High-ranking nobles and officials also constructed early mastabas, albeit smaller and less elaborate. The belief in an afterlife extended beyond the royal household, and these tombs sometimes contained chilling reminders of the fear-based culture. Scenes might depict the tomb owner receiving tribute from subordinates or smiting enemies, mirroring the king's iconography on a smaller scale. The officials, too, wanted to showcase their power.

Some of these tombs contained grave goods meant to protect the dead from malevolent spirits. Amulets shaped like the Udjat Eye (Eye of Horus) or protective deities, magical spells inscribed on labels, and even personal weapons served as barriers against ghosts or demons. Although many details of Early Dynastic religious practice remain unclear, it is certain that these people believed the afterlife was full of potential dangers. They needed magical tools to defend themselves—and their fear of being attacked in the next world was as real as their fear of earthly enemies.

3.10 The Desert as a Realm of Spirits

Many of the Early Dynastic cemeteries were located on the desert's edge. This boundary between the fertile Nile and the barren sands was deeply symbolic. Egyptians saw the desert as a place of wildness, inhabited by dangerous animals and possibly malevolent spirits. Burying the dead in the desert might have been a practical choice—it was dry, and floods did not reach there—but it also held spiritual meaning. The dryness of the desert helped preserve bodies, which was important for a successful afterlife. But it also placed the dead near a domain associated with fear and unpredictability.

People told stories about desert demons or ghosts that wandered among the dunes. Some believed that if the proper rituals were not performed, the dead might roam the desert, harassing the living. These tales encouraged families to pay for funerary rites, offerings, and prayers, reinforcing the power of the priesthood and the monarchy. Anyone who risked skipping these services not only jeopardized the soul of the deceased but also endangered themselves, for a restless spirit could bring misfortune.

3.11 Expanding the Pantheon: Early Gods and Their Terrifying Forms

During the Early Dynastic Period, the Egyptian pantheon began taking shape in recognizable ways. Deities like Horus, Seth, and Wadjit were already worshipped. Horus was especially significant, often identified with the king himself. Represented as a falcon, Horus was both majestic and predatory, implying that the king, as Horus on Earth, had a ruthless side. Seth, another important god, symbolized chaos and violence. Though he was demonized in later periods, in the Early Dynastic era, Seth could also be a protector under the right circumstances.

This dynamic pantheon gave religious justification for acts of violence. If the king was Horus, then crushing his enemies was as natural as a falcon hunting its prey. Priests and scribes wove frightening stories and symbols into religious texts, many of which have not survived but are hinted at in later inscriptions. Such stories reinforced the view that gods could be terrifying if angered. In turn, the king, as the gods' representative, wielded a fearsome power over both the living and the dead.

3.12 Graphic Images on Labels and Pottery

Much of what we know about early beliefs comes from small artifacts like ivory labels or decorated pottery shards found in royal tombs. Some show rows of captives with arms tied behind their backs, others display scenes of animals devouring men. Scholars debate whether these images were literal or symbolic. Either way, they painted a picture of a harsh world in which might often made right.

One famous item is the "Scorpion Macehead," which might represent a ruler known as the Scorpion King (though the details remain murky). The macehead features the king wearing a crown, holding a hoe for ceremonial purposes, and watching an irrigation or military event. Surrounding him are figures that could be enemies or subordinates. Scenes like this combine the king's role in providing life-giving water with his power to dominate and potentially kill. This duality, so central to Egyptian kingship, carried an undercurrent of dread. Even the gifts of the land were linked to the forceful presence of a divine king.

3.13 Threatening the Beyond: Unwritten Curses

While direct textual curses from the Early Dynastic Period are rare, the principle of magical protection and retribution likely existed in some form. Later in Egyptian history, we find numerous tomb inscriptions warning trespassers of dire consequences, such as being seized by the guardians of the afterlife or having their souls devoured by monstrous deities. Scholars believe these ideas had roots in earlier times. The presence of protective amulets, carved images of aggressive gods, and elaborate burial rites all suggest that the notion of a tomb's sanctity was already well-established.

Even if specific curses were not written down, the symbolic language spoke volumes. The repeated portrayal of the king smiting enemies, the arrangement of human sacrifices around his tomb, and the use of dangerous animals (like serpents and crocodiles) as protective motifs served as a warning. Harm the royal tomb or steal from the burial chambers, and you may unleash supernatural doom upon yourself.

3.14 Daily Life and Fear of the State

Beyond the grand tombs and palaces, ordinary people also felt the weight of Early Dynastic authority. Farmers, artisans, and laborers had to give a portion of their produce or crafts to support the temples and the royal household. Those who could not pay risked punishments. Military service might be forced upon young men, particularly during campaigns or major construction projects. In a world with no modern communication tools, rumors of harsh reprisals spread quickly. People might have heard tales of entire villages punished for failing to meet quotas.

There were also localized priests and officials who wielded considerable power over their districts. These individuals collected taxes, organized building crews, and enforced the king's demands. Corruption could run rampant, and an official might frame someone for withholding tribute just to seize land or valuables. The fear of arbitrary punishment by local authorities added to the general sense of unease. Common folk might rely on local shrines or household gods for protection, but ultimately, the king's command overshadowed all.

3.15 Ceremonies and Festivals with a Dark Edge

The Early Dynastic kings celebrated festivals that could have frightening elements. One such celebration might have been a renewal rite for the king, symbolizing his continued strength to rule. This could include a procession displaying conquered enemies, or a symbolic reenactment of the king defeating the forces of chaos. Animals might be sacrificed, and the public could witness these bloody events as proof of the king's power. Children watched with wide eyes, learning early that their ruler maintained cosmic order through violence.

Some festivals focused on the dead king, ensuring his spirit's smooth transition to the afterlife. While these ceremonies had joyous aspects (feasting and drinking), they also included solemn moments where priests invoked protective gods and chanted spells to ward off evil spirits. In the flickering torchlight, with incense filling the air, these chants could be eerie and mesmerizing. The line between divine mercy and divine wrath was thin—a small mistake during the ritual might bring calamity.

3.16 The Changing Face of Burial

By the end of the Second Dynasty, major shifts were underway in how Egyptians prepared tombs. Mastabas grew in complexity, featuring multiple rooms, offering chambers, and false doors where the deceased's spirit (the ka) was believed to enter to receive offerings. The living left food, drink, and incense to appease the ka. If neglected, it was feared the spirit might grow angry and haunt the living. This system of regular offerings gave priests an enduring role as mediators between the living and the dead.

We also see a move away from actual human sacrifice toward more symbolic burial customs. Wooden or clay figurines began to appear in tombs, representing servants or guardians. These figurines were meant to come to life in the afterworld to serve the deceased, thus removing the "need" for real human attendants. Still, the memory of earlier, more direct methods lingered. The knowledge that not long ago entire groups of people might be buried with a ruler added a grim layer to the evolving funerary tradition.

3.17 Shifting Capitals and Centers of Power

During the Early Dynastic Period, the main seat of power shifted to Memphis, a city near the southern apex of the Nile Delta. Memphis grew into a bustling metropolis, home to the royal court and numerous officials. This centralization helped the king extend control throughout the land more effectively. Temples and royal workshops in Memphis produced fine pottery, stone vessels, and jewelry, much of which found its way into tombs.

Yet, no matter how splendid the city became, there was always an undercurrent of fear. The monarchy's main goal was to maintain a stable society that honored the king as a living god. This stability hinged on collecting taxes, building monuments, and keeping the population under strict control. Rebellion or civil disorder could be met with lethal force. The bodies of executed rebels might be thrown into common graves without proper rites, an ultimate punishment for Egyptians who believed that a good afterlife required a respectful burial.

3.18 Rise of a Distinct Ruling Class

By the end of the Early Dynastic Period, Egyptian society was structured more rigidly than before. A distinct ruling class composed of royal family members, high priests, and top officials benefited from privileged lives. They built fine houses near the palaces, consumed imported luxuries, and prepared elaborate tombs. Meanwhile, the lower classes worked the fields, served in the army, or toiled on state building projects.

Though not everyone lived in daily terror, the threat of losing favor, land, or life hung over any who dared to challenge the system. The priests often reinforced this social order by teaching that the gods had established the king's rule. Thus, even the slight whisper of treason or blasphemy could ruin a person's life. Some might flee to remote areas to escape heavy taxes or forced labor, but the desert was perilous, and living away from the protective reach of the Nile was itself a dangerous gamble.

3.19 Echoes of Dread and the Path Ahead

As the Early Dynastic Period moved toward the era we call the Old Kingdom, the building blocks of Egyptian civilization were firmly in place: a god-king, a centralized administration, and advanced burial customs that combined awe-inspiring craftsmanship with unsettling traditions. Fear was woven into nearly every aspect of life, from the possibility of forced sacrifice at a king's funeral to the daily risk of punishment for minor offenses.

At the same time, the Egyptians believed in a cosmic order that balanced fear with hope. The annual Nile floods brought new life each year, demonstrating that the land could be generous. Religious rituals assured them that if they performed their duties, the gods would provide. Still, the capacity for state violence lingered at the edges of every celebration and festival, reminding people that their king ruled by both divine grace and tangible force.

CHAPTER 4

Step Pyramids, Human Sacrifices, and the Afterlife

The **Old Kingdom** of Egypt (c. 2686–2181 BCE) is known for its monumental pyramids and the evolution of a highly organized state. It began soon after the Early Dynastic Period and lasted until the decline that set in around the First Intermediate Period. This chapter focuses on the early Old Kingdom years, especially the reign of King Djoser and the creation of Egypt's first step pyramid at Saqqara. We will explore how the construction of these grand tombs was tied to labor, fear, and rumors of human sacrifice, as well as how the Egyptian view of the afterlife grew increasingly complex—and, for some, terrifying.

4.1 Djoser and the Vision of Imhotep

The first notable king of the Third Dynasty was **Djoser** (sometimes spelled Netjerikhet). He is remembered primarily for his grand tomb, the Step Pyramid at Saqqara. This pyramid did not emerge from nothing; it was built on earlier traditions of mastabas. However, the Step Pyramid was a groundbreaking concept in scale and design. The mind behind it was the king's architect and high official **Imhotep**, who would later be deified for his wisdom.

To create this massive structure, workers had to cut and transport thousands of stone blocks. The building site became a bustling hive of activity. Legends about forced labor linger around such projects, and while modern scholars debate whether the workforce was enslaved or paid in rations, it is certain that Djoser's authority—both practical and supernatural—compelled people to labor in large numbers. Many common Egyptians might have feared the consequences of refusing royal summons. Stories circulated of workers vanishing for disobedience or being severely punished if they tried to flee their duties.

4.2 From Mastaba to Pyramid

Before Djoser's Step Pyramid, royal tombs were typically mastabas—low, flat-roofed structures with sloping sides. Imhotep's innovation was to stack multiple mastaba shapes one on top of the other, forming a six-tiered pyramid. This new shape had a deeply symbolic meaning for ancient Egyptians. It could represent a staircase to the heavens or a representation of the primeval mound from which the world was thought to have emerged in Egyptian creation myths.

For the people who worked and lived around this project, the structure itself might have seemed both awe-inspiring and ominous. Never before had they seen such a huge building of stone. The ramp systems, wooden scaffolding, and sheer size of the workforce were all new. Accidents likely happened—stone blocks slipping, scaffolds collapsing—adding a real layer of mortal danger. Some workers might have whispered that the project was cursed or that the spirits of the desert resented disturbing the land on such a massive scale.

4.3 Rumors of Ongoing Human Sacrifice

While large-scale human sacrifice in royal burials seems to have mostly died out after the early dynasties, rumors persisted. Some believed the Step Pyramid demanded blood offerings to guarantee its success. These rumors might have grown out of older traditions or local superstitions. In reality, archaeological evidence does not show clear mass human burials linked to Djoser's pyramid. However, there are some intriguing finds: burial pits containing dismembered animal bones and the remains of smaller-scale sacrifices. It's also possible that criminals or war captives were quietly executed in ceremonies connected to the construction or dedication of the pyramid, although direct evidence is slim.

Such tales, whether true or exaggerated, spread fear. Workers might have told each other frightening stories around campfires at night, describing how the spirits of the newly dead haunted the partially built tunnels. The threat of royal power was never far away, and any suspicion of sabotage or rebellion on the construction site could lead to severe punishment. These stories added to the sense that building a pharaoh's tomb was more than just labor—it was a brush with mystical forces far beyond ordinary human control.

4.4 The Pyramid Complex: Maze of Passages and Traps

Djoser's Step Pyramid was not just a single structure. Surrounding it was a vast complex of courtyards, temples, and ceremonial buildings made to serve the king in the afterlife. This was the first large-scale stone complex in Egypt. Beneath the pyramid ran a labyrinth of corridors, chambers, and trap-filled passageways meant to protect the king's burial chamber. Stone blocks, secret doors, and possibly concealed pits guarded the final resting place. The idea was to thwart potential grave robbers, who, if caught, might face both mortal punishment and supernatural wrath.

The underground chambers were adorned with blue faience tiles meant to resemble the reed-mat walls of a royal palace. This attempt to replicate the living world below ground highlights the Egyptians' belief that life continued after death, in a realm that mirrored earthly existence. To modern eyes, this concept can be both fascinating and eerie. The idea that the king would continue his rule in a vast, underground fortress evoked images of a ghostly monarchy, ruling over spirits and the undead.

4.5 Expanding the Afterlife Beliefs

During Djoser's time, Egyptians refined the notion that the king was not only a divine figure on earth but also ascended to a celestial realm after death. Many texts from this era have not survived, but later Old Kingdom inscriptions, such as the Pyramid Texts, shed light on these beliefs. They describe the king's soul traveling to the sky, merging with the sun god Ra or the star gods.

The ordinary person's afterlife was far less certain in official doctrine. Some believed that only the king (and maybe select nobles) truly achieved eternal life among the gods, while others' afterlife was unclear. This inequality could be frightening. A common laborer, seeing the enormous resources poured into the king's tomb, might wonder if he and his family had any hope of a peaceful eternity. Over time, the concept of an afterlife open to more people began to develop, but in the early Old Kingdom, the king's exclusive route to immortality underlined the gap between royal privilege and the rest of society.

4.6 Labor Forces, Hierarchy, and Fear

To construct something as enormous as the Step Pyramid complex, Djoser needed an efficient system to manage the workforce. The state collected grain as taxes, distributing it back as rations to laborers. Skilled workers such as stonemasons, architects, and overseers received better provisions and living conditions than the masses. These specialists formed a hierarchy under the watchful eye of the king's appointed administrators.

Workplace discipline could be severe. Overseers had the power to mete out corporal punishment, beatings, or docked rations for those who slacked or disobeyed orders. The threat of punishment alone must have motivated many to keep laboring under the blazing sun, hauling heavy stones day after day. Some might have viewed Djoser as a benevolent figure if he provided enough food and security, but the system behind him remained strict and often harsh.

4.7 The Role of Imhotep and Religious Authority

Imhotep, who oversaw the Step Pyramid's design, became a legendary figure. He was not only the pyramid's architect but also served as a high priest of the sun god Ra at Heliopolis. Over centuries, Egyptians revered Imhotep as a wise man, eventually worshipping him as a god of medicine and knowledge.

Still, the worship of Imhotep in later periods should not mask the fact that during the Step Pyramid's construction, he wielded significant power. He could command large numbers of laborers and direct resources as he saw fit. The union of architectural skill and religious authority meant that no one dared to challenge his decisions openly. If someone opposed Imhotep, they risked offending not just the king but the gods themselves. Whether Imhotep used fear tactics is not recorded, but in an environment where the entire state believed in divine punishment, even unspoken threats could be potent.

4.8 Construction Accidents and Supernatural Blame

Building a pyramid was extremely dangerous work. Falling stones, collapses, and accidents with tools could easily maim or kill. When accidents happened, some workers may have blamed malevolent spirits or a curse tied to disturbing the sacred ground. Others might have seen it as punishment from the king's protective deities for laziness or misconduct.

Priests might then perform rituals to appease the angry forces, slaughtering animals or burning incense to cleanse the site. A few scapegoats—workers suspected of wrongdoing—could face dismissal or worse. These events might deepen the sense of dread, as people became convinced that invisible powers hovered around the construction site, waiting to strike anyone who did not follow orders or show proper respect.

4.9 The Sed Festival and Renewing Kingly Might

The Old Kingdom rulers celebrated a ceremony known as the **Sed Festival**, typically held after a king had ruled for many years. This festival was meant to rejuvenate the king's strength and demonstrate his continued ability to govern. Djoser likely celebrated such a festival in a special courtyard at Saqqara, built specifically for this purpose. During the ceremonies, the king would run a symbolic race, prove his physical vitality, and perhaps reenact mythical battles against the forces of chaos.

While the festival probably included feasts and music, it also carried hints of danger. Sacrificial offerings to the gods—animals, produce, and possibly human captives—demonstrated the king's power. Spectators would watch the king in ritual garb, possibly wearing masks or special crowns that portrayed the gods' fierceness. The message was clear: the king was chosen by divine forces, and no mortal could stand against him. Anyone tempted to revolt might recall the cruelty displayed against sacrificial victims during the Sed Festival.

4.10 Burials of the Nobles: Imitating Royal Terror

Not only Djoser but also high-ranking officials and nobles began building more complex tombs during the early Old Kingdom. These mastabas at Saqqara sometimes included small chapels where relatives could leave offerings. Walls inside might depict the tomb owner hunting, farming, or receiving tribute from servants. Though less grand than the Step Pyramid, some tombs rivaled small temples in scale.

The decorations could include scenes of punishments inflicted on disobedient workers or foreign captives. Such images mirrored the royal iconography of smiting enemies. Nobles did this to associate themselves with the king's right to exert violence. By copying this visual language, they reinforced a society in which terror was an acceptable instrument of authority. Even in death, these officials wanted to show they held power—both in the mortal world and the next.

4.11 Evolving Mortuary Rituals and Spells

As the idea of an elaborate afterlife for the king took hold, mortuary rituals grew more complex. Priests performed daily offerings of food and drink at mortuary temples attached to or near the pyramid complexes. Over time, specialized spells, prayers, and incantations developed—precursors to the later "Pyramid Texts" that would appear in the pyramids of the Fifth and Sixth Dynasties. Some of these early incantations likely described the king's ascension to the heavens and his transformation into a star or a companion of Ra.

These texts often included protective spells against the dangers lurking in the afterlife—serpents, demons, and vengeful spirits. The possibility of malevolent entities in the underworld added a new layer of fear to funeral rites. Priests reassured the living that proper rituals and offerings would keep the king safe. Yet, there was also an implicit warning: if the living failed in their responsibilities, if they did not maintain the correct ceremonies, they too might face supernatural consequences.

4.12 The Step Pyramid as a Cultural Symbol

Djoser's pyramid complex influenced subsequent kings to try even more ambitious projects, leading eventually to the Great Pyramid at Giza. The Step Pyramid, however, retained a special aura as the first large stone monument of Egypt. Over centuries, people told legends of hidden chambers filled with treasures, secret passages guarded by curses, and even monstrous creatures set to devour intruders.

While these legends may be later inventions or exaggerations, they speak to the lasting impression the Step Pyramid made on Egyptian consciousness. To see such a massive structure rising out of the desert must have conjured both pride in human achievement and fear of the monumental forces—divine and kingly—that made it possible. The pyramid became a stage for religious ceremonies, a storehouse for the dead king's goods, and a statement about the reach of royal power, both in life and after death.

4.13 Worker Settlements and Control

Archaeological evidence suggests that workers lived in organized communities near the pyramid site. These settlements had housing, bakeries, and breweries to keep laborers fed. Skilled artisans might have lived in slightly better conditions, while unskilled laborers resided in crowded quarters. The state kept track of rations, attendance, and productivity, using administrators who reported up the chain of command.

People in these camps were under constant supervision. Overseers could report any complaints or dissent. If workers formed any conspiracies or spoke ill of the king, they risked arrest or worse. The environment encouraged silence and obedience. This atmosphere of control was vital to completing massive building projects. Modern estimates suggest that the workforce on a pyramid site could fluctuate from a few thousand to tens of thousands during peak seasons, making discipline a critical concern for the royal administration.

4.14 Tales of Tomb Robbers and Cursed Fates

Even though the Step Pyramid had intricate defenses, tomb robbing became a concern as soon as valuables were placed within. Ancient Egyptians faced severe penalties if caught stealing from tombs. The fear of curses may have started informally: rumors spread that those who entered the sacred domain uninvited would suffer plagues, madness, or be pursued by vengeful spirits. Over time, these rumors became part of the culture surrounding pyramid sites.

Though there is little direct evidence of explicit "curses" written inside Djoser's pyramid, the tradition of cursed tombs would become more explicit in later centuries. Still, the idea likely existed in an unwritten form during this period, reinforced by the dramatic architecture meant to lock out intruders. For many, the threat of an otherworldly curse was as intimidating as the king's earthly punishments.

4.15 Human Remains and Ritual Offerings

In the vicinity of the Step Pyramid complex, archaeologists have discovered burial pits containing both human and animal remains. The human remains do not appear to belong to large-scale retainer sacrifices like those in early dynasties. Instead, they might be individuals buried nearby for protective or cultic reasons. Some might have been priests, officials, or workers who died during the project. Their proximity to the king's monument indicates a belief that lying in the king's shadow granted a spiritual advantage—or perhaps they were sacrificed in smaller rituals lost to history.

Animal bones—mainly cattle, sheep, and birds—have been found in refuse pits, suggesting regular offerings and feasts during the construction. Meat was likely sacrificed to the gods or to the spirit of the king, then distributed among the workers. Some might see these feasts as joyous communal events. Yet, the ever-present possibility that certain rites could involve more sinister acts kept an air of tension around the site.

4.16 The King as a Demigod: Fading Human Boundaries

By the time of Djoser, the Egyptian king was no longer simply a chieftain with a connection to the divine. He was now widely regarded as a **demigod on Earth**, a living link between humans and the pantheon. This shift meant that disloyalty to the king was not just a social or political crime; it was an offense against the cosmic order. Such beliefs justified extreme punishments and deterred potential rebels.

Priests and scribes played a big role in perpetuating this ideology. They wrote hymns and inscriptions praising the king's divine birth and magical powers. In a world where literacy was limited to an elite few, scribes held a monopoly on crafting the official narrative. The common population, hearing these tales read aloud during festivals, would have little reason to doubt them—especially when the largest man-made structure they had ever seen stood as proof of the king's might.

4.17 The Scariness of Divine Judgment

As the Old Kingdom advanced, the idea that the gods judged a person's deeds after death started to crystallize. While this concept became more explicit in later texts, its roots were visible in the Step Pyramid era. For the average person, the fear of divine judgment could be real, but for the king, it was believed he would seamlessly join the gods. This privilege, again, highlighted the vast gap between the ruler and his subjects.

If an individual was accused of stealing from the pyramid site or disrespecting the king's cult, priests might warn that the gods would punish them in the afterlife. Perhaps their heart would be found wanting on the scales of judgment, or their spirit would be devoured by monstrous deities. Though the details of this postmortem punishment are more documented in later sources, the seeds of that belief likely caused unease among Old Kingdom workers who toiled under strict oversight.

4.18 Builders or Slaves? The Debate

Modern scholars debate whether the laborers who built the pyramids were slaves, conscripted workers, or relatively free farmers working off their taxes during the Nile's inundation season. The truth likely varied by time, place, and individual circumstances. Some workers might have been respected artisans who took pride in contributing to the king's monument, receiving better food and lodging than they could normally secure. Others, especially those who violated laws, might have been forced to work under threat of punishment.

In any case, the scale of control was immense. The royal administration decided who worked on the pyramid, how long they worked, and what they received in exchange. This centralized system maintained its grip through fear of fines, beatings, or more severe penalties. Even if some laborers believed they were serving a higher purpose, an undercurrent of dread persisted—fear of injury, fear of spiritual consequences, and fear of the king's wrath if standards were not met.

4.19 Completion and Grand Burial

When Djoser died, his body was prepared for burial in the Step Pyramid's central chamber, far beneath the towering stone levels. Priests likely performed elaborate rituals, anointing the corpse with oils and resins, wrapping it in fine linens, and placing it in a sarcophagus. Grave goods, including food, clothing, jewelry, and ritual objects, surrounded him. Even though direct references to large-scale retainer sacrifice are absent, smaller-scale rituals might have taken place—perhaps an offering of animals, or possibly human attendants if older traditions lingered in hidden corners of the realm.

Once sealed, the king's tomb was meant to remain inviolate for eternity. Over generations, though, tomb robbers and natural wear took their toll. Even so, the Step Pyramid endured as a testament to the synergy of fear, faith, and architectural genius. Its rising tiers symbolized Djoser's ambition to join the gods, and the labyrinth beneath it reminded everyone how far the state was willing to go to protect the king's spirit.

CHAPTER 5

Old Kingdom Monuments and the Frightening Side of Pyramid Building

The Old Kingdom (c. 2686–2181 BCE) of Ancient Egypt is often called the "Age of the Pyramids." This period saw the rise of the most iconic monuments in Egyptian history. After Djoser's success at Saqqara, kings continued pushing architectural boundaries, eventually leading to the massive pyramids at Giza. These structures remain famous for their grandeur and complexity. Yet behind the glory lies a darker story of extreme labor demands, rigid social control, harsh punishments, and a deep fear of displeasing both the king and the gods. This chapter will examine the **4th Dynasty**—the era when the biggest pyramids were built—and reveal the frightening aspects of pyramid building and life during this golden yet often grim age.

5.1 The 3rd Dynasty's Legacy and the Path to Giza

The end of the 3rd Dynasty was shaped by King Djoser's Step Pyramid at Saqqara. His architect, Imhotep, had shown Egyptians that building with stone in grand shapes could strengthen the king's image. After Djoser, successors like Sekhemkhet and Khaba also worked on step pyramids, though some remain incomplete or lost to time. These projects created a sense of competition among future kings: each new ruler wanted to outdo the previous one, demonstrating greater power and divine favor.

Fear played a part in this rivalry. A king who failed to expand monuments or maintain the labor force risked losing respect among nobles and priests. People might question whether he was truly favored by the gods. This pressure pushed kings toward bigger, more ambitious building schemes, which in turn required more laborers, higher taxes, and tougher oversight.

5.2 Sneferu and the Search for the Perfect Pyramid

The 4th Dynasty began with **King Sneferu** (c. 2613–2589 BCE). He was a prolific builder who oversaw the construction of at least three major pyramids. Early in his reign, Sneferu built the **Meidum Pyramid**, which started as a step pyramid but was later modified into a smooth-sided form. Its collapse—at least a partial one—might have happened not long after construction or in a later period, but stories of the failure spread. Workers and officials would have viewed any structural problems as a bad omen. Some might have blamed disloyalty among laborers, insufficient offerings to the gods, or curses from disturbed tombs.

Undeterred, Sneferu built the **Bent Pyramid** at Dahshur. It began rising at one angle, then suddenly changed mid-way, giving its upper part a bent shape. Scholars suggest that cracks or instability in the structure forced a sudden shift in plans. Egyptians of the time might have whispered that the pyramid's odd angle came from supernatural wrath—perhaps the spirits of the desert objected to such a giant edifice, or the gods signaled their displeasure with the king's methods. Determined to have a perfect monument, Sneferu went on to build the **Red Pyramid**, also at Dahshur, which emerged as the first successful smooth-sided pyramid. This final triumph showed that, despite setbacks and whispered fears, the king's will could prevail.

Still, each project demanded huge amounts of stone, labor, and resources. Sneferu's building frenzy likely put great strain on the population. Tax burdens rose, and labor conscription expanded. Many peasants found themselves forced to leave their fields for months, if not years, to haul massive limestone blocks in scorching heat. Overseers held the power to punish or even kill those who resisted. Rumors of people disappearing into desert quarries or being beaten to death for slow work added to the fear permeating everyday life.

5.3 The Labor System: Recruiting and Controlling Workers

Organizing labor was one of the biggest challenges for the Old Kingdom state. Large teams of workers—sometimes thousands—were needed to quarry stone, transport it by boat or sled, and carefully shape and stack it. Officials kept detailed accounts of worker numbers, rations, and tasks. Skilled laborers, such as stonecutters and masons, received better treatment. They often lived in slightly more comfortable settlements, ate more nutritious food, and sometimes earned prestige by serving the king's project directly. Unskilled workers, on the other hand, bore the heaviest burdens, pulling blocks with ropes or pushing them on wooden rollers.

Fear was a key tool for ensuring productivity. If someone complained too openly or tried to shirk duties, they could face severe punishments—beatings, reduced food rations, or even imprisonment. There are depictions in later tomb paintings of overseers with sticks, striking at laborers who appear to be slacking. While we do not have the exact images for the 4th Dynasty, it is likely that such methods existed at Giza as well. Rumors about "vanishing men" who dared to question the pyramid projects would have spread, reinforcing a culture of silent obedience.

5.4 King Khufu and the Great Pyramid's Shadow

Khufu (also known as Cheops), son of Sneferu, took the throne around 2589 BCE. He commissioned the largest pyramid ever built in Egypt, now known as the **Great Pyramid of Giza**. Rising to about 146 meters (originally) and consisting of an estimated 2.3 million stone blocks, it was a demonstration of raw power and logistic mastery.

For many Egyptians, the Great Pyramid might have been a stunning source of pride. But for those conscripted to work on it, it could be a **nightmare**. Records do not survive from Khufu's era that detail the building process. Later Greek writers, however, passed down stories—possibly embellished—of harsh labor conditions and even cruelty under Khufu's reign. Herodotus, writing centuries later, claimed that Khufu shut down temples, forced people to labor en masse, and subjected women to degrading tasks to fund his projects. Although these accounts may be exaggerated, they suggest that **fear** was central to Khufu's leadership style in popular memory.

The structure itself likely inspired supernatural awe. Even today, the scale of the Great Pyramid is hard to fathom. In ancient times, many believed it required not just human effort but possibly magical help. Some might have claimed that spirits or djinn (to use a later term) carried the blocks or that the king used secret spells to move stone. Anyone crossing the king in such a quest risked not only earthly punishment but also curses from beyond. Rumors of curses on those who harmed the pyramid's construction workers or defiled the site may have kept both laborers and local officials in line.

5.5 Giza Plateau: A Complex of Royal Authority

Khufu's pyramid was not alone. Over time, the Giza plateau gained two more major pyramids—built by **Khafre** and **Menkaure**—as well as queens' pyramids, mastaba tombs for nobles, and the **Great Sphinx**. This entire area became a stage for royal funerary rituals. The Sphinx, carved from limestone bedrock, had the body of a lion and a human head, usually identified as Khafre's. While modern viewers see it as a symbol of Egyptian grandeur, to an ancient peasant, it might have seemed like a **fierce guardian** capable of punishing intruders. Myths could easily form about the Sphinx awakening at night or devouring those who dared to trespass in the king's domain.

The tomb complexes at Giza were guarded by priests and necropolis officials, who performed daily rituals to feed and sustain the deceased kings' spirits. Strict rules governed who could enter certain areas, and the penalty for violating these rules was often death. Once again, the fear of curses or vengeful ghosts added to the sense of danger. Robbing or disturbing a royal tomb was one of the worst offenses imaginable. Even centuries later, tomb robbers rarely dared to break into these massive pyramids because they believed monstrous guardians or magical traps awaited inside.

5.6 Overseeing the Projects: Power and Corruption

Administering the Giza building sites was a massive undertaking. **Viziers** (the highest-ranking officials under the king) and other nobles supervised various departments—grain collection, labor allocation, tool production, and shipping. Because these men had great power, they often inspired fear in the local population. A single official could demand that dozens of farmers leave their fields to cut stone. If a local village refused, the official had the authority to punish or replace the village head. Nobles also controlled the distribution of rations. In times of shortage, corruption could doom entire families to starvation if they fell out of favor.

Such officials sometimes used intimidation to protect their own positions. They might accuse rivals of plotting against the king or speak of curses that would befall anyone who disobeyed "the will of the pharaoh." In truth, some of these claims were just political maneuvers, but in a deeply religious society, people took them seriously. The line between real spiritual danger and manufactured threats blurred, allowing the ruling class to maintain control.

5.7 Workers' Settlements and the Challenge of Living Conditions

Excavations at Giza in modern times have revealed traces of **workers' settlements**—clusters of dormitory-like structures, bakeries, breweries, and healing areas. While these findings suggest that the workers might not have been simple slaves in chains, the conditions still seemed harsh. There was a strict hierarchy: skilled laborers got better rations and lodging, while the unskilled slept in crowded quarters. Injuries were common—crushed limbs, broken bones, and accidents involving heavy stone blocks.

The fear of injury was real. A hurt laborer might lose the ability to work and thus receive fewer rations. With no social safety net beyond small local charities or temple offerings, a laborer's entire family could starve. Overseers sometimes spread rumors that injuries happened to those who **lacked faith** in the king's divine mission. This blame shifted responsibility away from the dangers of building giant stone monuments and placed it on the spiritual devotion of the workers themselves.

5.8 Tomb Art and Frightening Scenes

While many tomb paintings from the Old Kingdom focus on pleasant scenes—hunting in the marshes, feasting, and life along the Nile—some images hint at the darker sides of life. For instance, reliefs and statuary sometimes show guards with clubs, subjugated enemies, or lines of bound captives. These could be foreigners taken in military campaigns or locals who rebelled against the king's demands. The unspoken message was clear: disobedience led to humiliation and possibly death.

Additionally, some funerary texts, though still developing in this period, included references to sinister creatures in the afterlife. **Serpents, vultures, and fierce netherworld animals** could attack a soul that did not have the right spells or protective amulets. While these texts were primarily for the king and elite, rumors among the common people likely inflated such tales into vivid nightmares of monstrous guardians roaming the deserts around the pyramids. A child living near Giza might hear ghost stories that if you wandered too close to the tombs, a spirit could snatch you away.

5.9 Khafre and the Sphinx: More Than a Monument

Khafre, following Khufu, built the second-largest pyramid at Giza and commissioned the Great Sphinx. This lion-bodied statue with a man's head was possibly a literal fusion of royal and solar power. Egyptian religion often combined animal traits with human forms to represent aspects of the divine. A lion's strength was well-known; many children grew up hearing tales of lions in the desert that could tear a person apart. Grafting a king's head onto that body created an image that demanded **both reverence and dread**.

Cults around the Sphinx might have performed offerings, believing it to be a living divine presence, or at least a powerful statue that could intercede with the gods. Some also believed that the Sphinx guarded secret chambers beneath the plateau. This belief might have been enough to keep tomb robbers away. Over time, wind-blown sand partially buried the Sphinx. Workers or priests who tried to remove the sand might feel uneasy, thinking they were disturbing a living guardian. The threat of curses—though rarely inscribed in stone—kept fear alive.

5.10 Menkaure and Shifts in Pyramid Size

The last of the three main Giza pyramids was built by **Menkaure** (also known as Mykerinos), who came after Khafre. His pyramid was smaller, which might suggest a change in resources or a deliberate choice. While he still aimed for a grand monument, the downward shift in scale hinted that maintaining gigantic projects was proving harder over time. Some sources suggest Menkaure was considered a kinder ruler, but little direct evidence remains. Even if he was more lenient, the system of forced labor and high taxation continued, as the entire Old Kingdom economy was tied to pyramid building.

Because Menkaure's pyramid was not as large, rumors circulated about why. Some said it was the result of curses that haunted the bigger pyramids. Others claimed the land's resources had finally run thin or that spiritual balance demanded a reduction in the project's size. Regardless of the reason, many commoners likely felt relief that their labor might be less intense. Yet, fear of punishment for disobedience remained, and the structure was still massive by normal standards.

5.11 The Pyramid Towns and Strict Social Control

Around Giza and other pyramid sites, "pyramid towns" emerged—settlements dedicated to maintaining the king's cult after his death. Priests, scribes, and workers lived there, continuing daily offerings in mortuary temples. This tradition shows how the Old Kingdom was not just about building a tomb and forgetting it; the king's spirit needed ongoing care. The presence of priests and officials also ensured a continuous local authority. Anyone living near these towns stayed within a **network of surveillance**. Village elders, local temple officials, and scribes all reported to the higher bureaucracy. Even small disputes could lead to accusations of wrongdoing against the crown if they threatened the supply lines for the pyramid or temple.

The fear of being denounced to the authorities for minor infringements kept people obedient. If a priest accused someone of not delivering enough grain to the mortuary temple, that person might be hauled before a local official. Penalties could range from forced labor to physical punishment or confiscation of property. Such tight control might have allowed for an efficient society in some ways, but it also fostered an environment of anxiety.

5.12 Religious Shifts: King as Son of Ra

During the 4th Dynasty, the relationship between the king and the sun god **Ra** grew stronger. Earlier kings were seen as incarnations of Horus, but by the time of Khufu and Khafre, there was a growing emphasis on the king as the **son of Ra**. This heightened the king's divine status. Sun temples began to appear, and solar worship took on greater importance in state rituals.

This change had scary implications for the population. If the king was the literal offspring of the supreme sun god, opposing him became an even graver sin. People feared cosmic retribution, not just from local or funerary gods but from the very sun in the sky. Droughts, sandstorms, or extremely hot seasons might be interpreted as the sun god's anger. Any sign of disloyalty to the king could be blamed for bringing about environmental curses.

5.13 Expanding Administration and Local Tensions

As the Old Kingdom progressed, the state's administrative reach expanded, dividing the land into numerous provinces called "nomes." Nomarchs governed these nomes on behalf of the king. Though they answered to the royal court, some nomarchs gained power over local populations, levying taxes and conscripting laborers for pyramid projects. Over time, they built their own tombs, seeking to emulate the king's monumental style, albeit on a smaller scale.

For commoners, it often felt like **there was no escape** from demands. Whether they worked directly on pyramid sites or in their home districts, they faced the threat of forced labor or heavy taxation. The fear of local nomarchs might have matched the fear of the king. If a nomarch demanded more taxes than the farmland could sustain, refusing could bring swift punishment—yet paying could lead to starvation. This pressure cooker scenario foreshadowed problems that would eventually shake the Old Kingdom's foundations.

5.14 Tales of Magicians and Dark Spells

Popular stories from later periods refer to **magicians** living in the time of Khufu and his successors. One tale speaks of a magician who could reattach a severed head to a goose and bring it back to life. Another mentions a powerful spell that parted the waters of a lake. While these are likely literary inventions from later centuries, they hint at a belief that the 4th Dynasty was a magical era—both wondrous and frightening. People might have believed that the king and his priests used dark spells to accomplish their building feats or to curse anyone who doubted the monarchy.

Such stories reinforced the sense that the pyramids at Giza were more than mere tombs; they were strongholds of mystical energy. Fearing curses, many locals might have avoided going near certain parts of the construction site at night. The desert, with its howling winds, took on an eerie quality near the towering silhouettes of the pyramids.

5.15 Growing Strains and Signs of Decline

Although the 4th Dynasty was a pinnacle of pyramid building, cracks eventually appeared in the Old Kingdom's system. The costs of maintaining huge royal projects, plus the rising influence of local officials, strained the central government's control. Some sources hint at tensions between the royal court and powerful nomarchs who were far from Memphis, the capital.

For the average person, these tensions could translate into confusion: one day, a local official demanded labor for a pyramid, the next day, rumors spread that another official was challenging the king's authority. The people caught in the middle had every reason to be afraid—supporting the wrong side could lead to severe repercussions. Even if large-scale rebellions did not erupt immediately, the seeds of disorder were being planted.

5.16 The Fifth Dynasty: Shifts in Royal Focus

By the 5th Dynasty, which followed the famed 4th, attention shifted from massive pyramids at Giza to sun temples and smaller pyramids. Kings like

Userkaf and Sahure built complexes with more emphasis on **Ra** worship. While these new pyramids were still impressive, they were not on the same scale as Khufu's. The state might have been trying to balance resources, focusing on religious activities rather than exclusively on colossal tombs.

Yet, the fear-based system continued. People still owed labor and taxes. Priests still warned of cosmic consequences for disloyalty. The royal court developed more elaborate funerary texts—**Pyramid Texts**—inscribed on the walls inside pyramids, describing the king's perilous journey through the underworld. For commoners, these texts were inaccessible, but rumors of their content spread. Stories of demons, traps, and monstrous guardians in the afterlife gained detail, enhancing the mystique of the king's tomb and discouraging any idea of disturbing it.

5.17 More Officials, More Confusion

The bureaucracy of the Old Kingdom grew further. Multiple layers of scribes, inspectors, and overseers managed everything from cattle counts to farmland surveys. While this system could be efficient, it was also open to abuse and corruption. A greedy official could squeeze peasants dry. People with minimal means to defend themselves might live in constant dread of tax hikes or forced relocations to labor sites.

Because the king was seen as a distant figure—part human, part god—the local officials often acted as the face of the state. Some took advantage, accumulating wealth and building large mastabas near Memphis or other key sites. Their tomb scenes portrayed them punishing "lazy" workers or defeating enemies, mimicking the king's iconography. This repeated emphasis on violence showed that, at all levels of society, fear was a standard method of command.

5.18 Late Old Kingdom: Seeds of Unrest

As the 5th and 6th Dynasties progressed, monuments became smaller, though still elaborate. More resources went into temple-building for the gods. This shift might reflect a weakening of the centralized monarchy. Also, the climate is believed by some scholars to have changed, causing lower Nile floods, less farmland productivity, and eventual famine in certain areas. If the land could not produce enough food, the king's ability to reward officials and feed laborers declined. Hungry populations are more likely to rebel or defy commands.

A once-mighty system that thrived on fear and forced labor began to wobble. People in the provinces might have questioned whether the king was losing divine favor. If the Nile refused to flood sufficiently, perhaps the sun god Ra was angry. Factions might have formed among priests, nomarchs, and the royal family. Everyone still professed loyalty to the king, but the tension was palpable, setting the stage for a dark chapter in Egypt's history.

5.19 The Final Pharaohs of the Old Kingdom and the Rumblings of Collapse

The 6th Dynasty saw the lengthy reign of **Pepi II**, who supposedly ruled for over 90 years. While that reign sounds grand, many records hint that central authority was fracturing during his later years. Nomarchs grew bolder, carving out local power bases. The king, aging and distant, might not have been able to maintain the same grip on the land as earlier rulers. Pyramid building continued but lacked the same intimidation factor of Khufu's Great Pyramid.

For ordinary Egyptians, this shift in power could be both a relief and a source of new terror. On one hand, if the central government was weak, perhaps the demands for labor and taxes lessened. On the other hand, local power struggles could erupt into violence. Without a strong central authority, peasants could be caught between warring local lords. The official ideology of fear—focused on the king's divine authority—now tangled with the real, unpredictable fear of civil strife.

CHAPTER 6

First Intermediate Period: Chaos and Fear

The **Old Kingdom** ended around 2181 BCE, giving way to what historians call the **First Intermediate Period** (c. 2181–2055 BCE). This era was marked by the collapse of strong central authority, the rise of local warlords, famine, and social upheaval. Written records from this period suggest a chaotic world where law and order broke down, tombs were robbed, and people lived in dread of violence from both fellow Egyptians and the unseen forces they believed roamed a land abandoned by the gods. This chapter examines the terrifying aspects of the First Intermediate Period: how a once-unified Egypt fell into disorder, and how fear ruled daily life during these troubled times.

6.1 The Downfall of the Old Kingdom

Though Pepi II of the 6th Dynasty may have enjoyed a long reign, the real power of the pharaoh had been draining away. Nomarchs, once mere representatives of the king in local districts, began acting independently. They passed down their offices to family members, building miniature "dynasties" in their nomes. Over time, this transformation shredded the concept of a single, divine ruler.

At the same time, weak Nile floods or shifts in climate led to **poor harvests**. Starvation became a real threat. People who once relied on the king's granaries for relief found little help if local officials hoarded supplies or simply did not have enough. Word spread that the gods had turned their backs on Egypt, punishing the land for unknown sins. Rumors of black magic or the wrath of neglected deities fueled anxiety, with people suspecting one another of bringing curses upon entire communities.

6.2 Fragmented Kingdoms and Rival Factions

Egypt broke into several power centers. In the north, based around Memphis and the Delta, some leaders claimed the title of pharaoh, while in the south, rival dynasties rose. The city of **Herakleopolis** in Middle Egypt emerged as a powerful kingdom, while Thebes in Upper Egypt also formed its own rule under local warlords or nomarchs who declared themselves kings. The central government was no longer able to unify these areas.

This fragmentation meant **constant conflict**. Local rulers raised small armies, either to defend their territory from neighbors or to seize better farmland and trade routes. Common people were drafted into these militias, forced to fight neighbors with whom they once traded or shared festival days. Stories of raids and massacres circulated widely, creating fear not just of foreign invaders but of fellow Egyptians. Farmers might wake to see a column of soldiers in the distance, uncertain if they were friend or foe.

6.3 Tomb Robbery and the Violation of Sacred Spaces

With the collapse of central authority, many tombs—once considered untouchable—were **robbed or desecrated**. Tomb robbery had existed even in stable times, but it was a severe crime usually punished harshly. Now, in the absence of a strong government, desperate people turned to looting for survival. They stripped tombs of gold, jewelry, and precious goods meant for the afterlife. Mummies were ripped apart in the search for hidden amulets or valuables. The act was considered not just theft, but a violation of sacred rites, sparking deep terror among those who believed in curses tied to disturbing the dead.

For the devout, this sacrilege was a sign that the world had gone mad. Priests and scribes lamented that the protective spells no longer held power, or that the gods themselves had abandoned Egypt in disgust. Tales of avenging spirits might have kept some robbers away, but hunger and poverty could override fear. This contributed to a general sense that no place, not even the resting sites of the revered dead, was safe.

6.4 The "Admonitions of Ipuwer": A Terrifying Picture

A famous text from this era, often referred to as the **"Admonitions of Ipuwer"**, paints a bleak picture of chaos. Although its dating and exact historical accuracy are debated, it is often associated with the First Intermediate Period's sense of collapse. The text describes a land in turmoil: foreigners roam freely, the Nile's waters are low, the rich become poor while the poor grow bold, and the natural order is overturned.

Lines from the text lament the lack of respect for tradition: "The tomb-chambers are laid bare, noblemen's tombs are rifled." It also speaks of violence: "Indeed, laughter has perished, it is no longer made; there is a groaning throughout the land." While these might be poetic flourishes, they capture the widespread fear and despair of a society losing its moral and religious anchors. People lived with the notion that their entire culture was unravelling, a terrifying thought for those who once believed in an unbreakable cosmic order.

6.5 Local Despots and their Brutal Rule

As the old monarchy faded, local warlords or nomarchs often ruled by **brutal force**. If a district had fertile lands, the ruler might demand heavy taxes from peasants, threatening to seize their children or burn their fields if they could not pay. Some warlords commanded gangs of armed men who extorted wealth from passing caravans. Foreign traders, once welcomed during the Old Kingdom, became targets for robbery or kidnapping.

Even religious institutions were not spared. Temples might be raided for their gold and precious offerings. Priests could be coerced into supporting a local strongman's claim to rulership. This breakdown of social norms spread **terror**. People could not trust the old channels of authority, nor could they rely on religious centers to remain safe havens. The moral world they once knew was crumbling.

6.6 Famine and Disease

The First Intermediate Period was also marked by **famine**. When the Nile floods were too low, crop yields plummeted. Grain stores vanished quickly, leaving entire communities starving. Malnutrition weakens immune systems, so

diseases would have been rampant in these overcrowded, poorly fed populations. Children and the elderly suffered most, dying in large numbers. The sight of emaciated bodies or the smell of decaying corpses could haunt survivors, fueling rumors that the gods were punishing the land.

Those with access to food often hoarded it or sold it at ruinous prices. The gap between the "haves" and "have-nots" widened, leading to more theft, violence, and social unrest. In some stories, neighbors turned against each other, families argued over food, and parents were forced to make desperate choices. Such dire situations heightened superstition and fear: many believed that only magic or divine intervention could save them from hunger and plague.

6.7 Religious Confusion and Syncretism

Before this period, religion was largely unified under the concept of a divine pharaoh maintaining Maat (cosmic order). Now, with multiple claimants to the throne, the **religious landscape** grew confused. Different regions emphasized different gods. Some local rulers promoted their own cults, claiming direct contact with a patron deity. The usual centralized temple organization began to fragment, and priests who once answered to Memphis now followed local lords.

For commoners, this chaos in religion was as frightening as the political breakdown. They asked: Which god should we pray to for the Nile's return? Which rite would keep disease away? The comforting predictability of state rituals, with the pharaoh at the helm, vanished. Many turned to local mystics, wandering holy men, or minor cults for answers. Some claimed to hold secret knowledge to appease the angry gods, selling amulets or charms. Fear of spiritual punishment grew stronger, as people believed a single wrong choice in worship could doom them further.

6.8 Rise of Banditry and Desert Threats

With fewer soldiers stationed at traditional outposts, **bandits** roamed the trade routes and desert edges. Caravan raids became common, and merchants had to hire their own guards or pay bribes to local warlords. The deserts, once a frontier zone controlled by the pharaoh's might, transformed into a realm of lawless raiders. Stories spread of caravans disappearing without a trace, their guards found slain or never found at all.

This insecurity also spilled into the Nile Valley. Travelers feared journeying from one nome to another, uncertain which local ruler's territory they might enter. At times, minor conflicts flared into larger skirmishes, with entire villages set ablaze. The sense that Egypt was under siege—from external threats, from internal warlords, even from spiritual forces—was widespread. People who once took pride in the safety and unity of the kingdom now hid behind makeshift walls, too afraid to venture far from home.

6.9 Art and Literature Reflecting Sorrow and Terror

Though many artistic and literary works from the First Intermediate Period were lost or destroyed, those that remain show a **shift in tone** from Old Kingdom optimism to despair and anxiety. Stelas from local rulers depict them not just as noble protectors, but as conquerors who boast of crushing enemies and pacifying rebellious subjects. Their language is harsher, their scenes more violent.

Some personal letters or inscriptions hint at sorrow over lost family members, fear of tomb robbers, and worry about the future. In place of grand hymns to the pharaoh, local scribes might compose laments about the lack of justice. The breakdown of the royal building projects also meant fewer large-scale monuments to show national unity. Small tombs or local chapels replaced grand pyramids, reflecting both limited resources and the precarious state of society.

6.10 Shifting Burial Customs: Survival Over Splendor

During the Old Kingdom, the wealthy built grand mastabas or pyramids. Now, with resources scarce and tomb robbery rampant, many families opted for **simpler burials**. They might inter their dead in common graves or small rock-cut tombs with modest goods—enough to show respect for the afterlife but not so lavish as to attract thieves.

Because fear of robbers was high, some people hid their tombs in remote cliffs or sealed them in ways meant to mislead looters. A few might have scrawled curses at the entrances, threatening any intruder with divine wrath. Whether these curses were believed to be effective or just a desperate gesture, they reflect the pervasive anxiety about losing one's final resting place. The cultural belief that a disturbed tomb could doom the soul to wander as a restless spirit intensified the dread of what was happening across the land.

6.11 The Role of Magic and Sorcery

As central religious authority weakened, **magic** and **sorcery** became more common in everyday life. People turned to local wise men, healers, or magicians for solutions to problems once addressed by temple rites. A mother might seek a protective amulet for her child, terrified of sickness or malicious spirits. A farmer might ask for a spell to protect his meager grain supply from thieves. But these practices also sparked suspicion. Anyone who possessed unusual charms or knowledge risked being labeled a sorcerer capable of bringing misfortune. Accusations of dark magic became a weapon in local feuds.

Stories spread about necromancers who could raise the dead to terrorize the living, or witches who could poison wells. Some towns might try to ban or expel such individuals, fearing the wrath of angry ghosts or gods. Once again, chaos and uncertainty fed fear, leading to superstition that sometimes exploded into violence against perceived "evil" practitioners.

6.12 Thebes and Herakleopolis: Clashing Centers

Two major powers rose during this period, each claiming the right to unite Egypt. In **Herakleopolis**, a dynasty controlling Middle and Lower Egypt vied for recognition. In **Thebes**, a southern dynasty led by warlike rulers sought to expand north. The rivalry between these two centers led to military campaigns and shifting alliances. Civilians caught in the path of these armies endured terror—looted homes, burned crops, forced conscription.

Leaders in both cities claimed divine backing for their cause. Herakleopolis had ancient ties to the Memphite tradition, while Thebes boasted devotion to the god Amun (though Amun's prominence would grow much larger in later periods). The competition might have included propaganda praising each side's devotion to the gods, painting the enemy as heretical or cursed. This propaganda fueled hatred, making the conflicts even more brutal.

6.13 Local Governors: Kings in All but Name

Outside the main contenders, many local governors acted like **small-scale kings** in their districts. They minted their own seals, built fortresses, and hosted lavish feasts to show power. They collected taxes for themselves rather than for any distant ruler. Some tried to maintain order, genuinely protecting their people from roving bandits or rival nomarchs. Others became tyrants, using fear to hoard wealth and crush opposition.

Commoners often had to weigh the risks: pledge loyalty to a local governor who might keep bandits at bay, or resist and risk being labeled a traitor. Betrayals were frequent; a nomarch might switch sides, proclaiming allegiance to Thebes one day, then Herakleopolis the next. In this environment, no one could be sure which leaders would remain in power. Families sometimes fled, seeking refuge in a more stable region or trying to migrate to Nubia or the oases, but those journeys held their own dangers.

6.14 The Fear of Being Forgotten

To Egyptians, memory was crucial to a good afterlife. During the Old Kingdom, a person's tomb would be maintained by priests or family members, ensuring their name stayed alive. But in the First Intermediate Period, entire families perished in famine, or were uprooted by war. Tombs fell into ruin or were looted. Many believed that their **souls would be doomed** if no one remembered their name or brought offerings. The terror of being forgotten—worse than death in Egyptian belief—stalked the land.

For a civilization that placed enormous value on funerary rites and the continuity of tradition, this breakdown was devastating. People who had once expected a secure afterlife now faced the real possibility of being buried in unmarked pits or left in the open. The social and spiritual safety nets had unraveled, leaving individuals to fend for themselves.

6.15 Attempts to Restore Order: Kings of Herakleopolis

Some rulers in Herakleopolis tried to restore a semblance of peace. They reorganized local administration, punished tomb robbers, and rebuilt damaged shrines. These kings argued that they were the rightful heirs to the Old Kingdom's legacy. They promoted religious festivals and presented themselves as protectors of tradition. Yet, their control was never absolute. Thebes in the south refused to bow. Smaller warlords still operated on the fringes, and famine lingered.

The Herakleopolitan kings might have used harsh measures to impose order. Tales describe entire villages burned for suspected rebellion, or dissidents crucified (or impaled) as warnings. Even if these accounts are embellished, the underlying truth is that local populations lived in constant dread. The same tactics of fear once used by a unified monarchy were now employed by multiple competing rulers, each claiming divine approval.

6.16 The Theban Challenge: Mentuhotep's Rise

In Thebes, a line of rulers grew in ambition, especially under **Mentuhotep II**. Determined to conquer the north, Mentuhotep II built up an army and launched campaigns against Herakleopolis and its allies. He claimed that the gods favored Thebes and that he alone could end the chaos. Propaganda from Theban scribes pictured him as a restorer of order, a champion who would crush the "wicked" Herakleopolitan kings.

The reality was brutal warfare. Cities surrendered or were taken by force; prisoners might be executed or enslaved. Families were torn apart; farmland was trampled by armies. Fear of Theban aggression spread among Herakleopolitan sympathizers. Thebes, too, might have felt fear—if they failed, their leaders would face harsh retribution. The entire land existed in a tense and bloody stalemate.

6.17 Bandits, Rebels, and Shattered Communities

As Thebes and Herakleopolis fought, smaller groups exploited the chaos. Bandits roamed, free of any central authority to stop them. In some districts, local militiamen turned into **raiders** themselves when they realized no one was watching. Real rebels who refused to recognize either side set up independent enclaves.

Communities broke apart. Market days that once brought prosperity now became risky gatherings where fights could break out. People feared traveling outside their villages. Disease spread quickly in the cramped conditions of temporary refuges or half-burned towns. Desperation drove some to **cannibalism** in the worst-hit areas, at least according to later, possibly exaggerated, accounts. Rumors of such acts magnified the sense of horror.

6.18 A Change in Beliefs: Democratization of the Afterlife

Interestingly, amid all this turmoil, religious ideas began to shift. The concept that **anyone** with the right knowledge, spells, and devotion could attain a blissful afterlife started to gain ground. No longer was the afterlife seen as primarily the domain of kings. This shift could reflect a desire for hope in a crumbling world: if the central monarchy was not stable, perhaps individuals could take responsibility for their own spiritual fate.

Yet, achieving a secure afterlife still required resources—for a coffin, for funerary texts, for a proper burial. This led to new forms of tomb decoration, with personal inscriptions and "Coffin Texts" that expanded upon older Pyramid Text themes. For many, though, the cost remained too high, and the fear of dying without proper rites haunted them. It was a small silver lining that religious possibilities were opening up, but it existed in a world overshadowed by violence and instability.

6.19 Paths to Reunification

Eventually, Theban rulers gained the upper hand. **Mentuhotep II** defeated his rivals, reuniting Egypt around 2055 BCE. He consolidated power and established what we now call the **Middle Kingdom**. Monuments from his reign celebrate the triumph of order over chaos, praising him as the deliverer who ended the dreadful First Intermediate Period. While fear did not vanish overnight, the reestablishment of a single authority reduced some of the immediate terrors of local warfare and famine.

For those who had lived through the turmoil, however, scars remained. Entire generations grew up knowing only a fragmented Egypt. The memory of tomb robberies, famine, and unchecked violence lingered. This collective trauma shaped the mindset of the Middle Kingdom, influencing how people related to the king, the gods, and each other. Fear as a ruling tool did not disappear, but it found new forms under the restored monarchy.

CHAPTER 7

Middle Kingdom: Tomb Robberies and Dark Rituals

When Egypt finally emerged from the chaos of the First Intermediate Period (c. 2181–2055 BCE), the land gradually consolidated under a single ruler once again. The Middle Kingdom (c. 2055–1650 BCE) began with the reunification led by pharaohs from Thebes, most notably **Mentuhotep II**. These new rulers worked to restore order and prosperity, but that did not eliminate fear and dark practices. Indeed, **tomb robberies** continued, **rituals** grew more intricate, and powerful **priesthoods** fought for influence. While the Middle Kingdom is often praised as a cultural renaissance, it also bore traces of cruelty and frightening beliefs that shaped people's daily lives.

7.1 Mentuhotep II and the Rebirth of a Centralized Authority

After years of division and violence during the First Intermediate Period, Mentuhotep II of Thebes succeeded in defeating rival rulers, especially those from Herakleopolis, and unified Egypt around 2055 BCE. Declaring himself the rightful pharaoh, he restored many functions of the old centralized government. For the average person, this reunification brought some relief. Armies no longer roamed the countryside in endless battles, and trade routes reopened. But consolidation under one leader did not mean an end to fear.

Mentuhotep II established a new capital in Thebes, or at least made it the religious heart of his kingdom, boosting local temples and priesthoods. To secure his power, he rewarded loyal officials with lands and privileges but also punished or exiled those who had sided with his enemies. Tales circulated of entire families dispossessed for having supported the Herakleopolitan kings. People were reminded that the pharaoh—while a bringer of unity—could still be ruthless. In Egyptian thought, the same king who saved them from chaos could employ harsh measures to maintain peace.

7.2 The Middle Kingdom's Ideology: A More Compassionate King?

Compared to the Old Kingdom's god-like rulers, the Middle Kingdom pharaohs sometimes depicted themselves in more human terms. Statues and reliefs show kings with thoughtful, even careworn expressions. Some historians interpret this as an effort to appear closer to the people. Pharaohs like **Senusret I** and **Senusret III** introduced legal reforms, regulated taxes more evenly, and tried to manage officials more carefully.

Yet, fear remained a political tool. While the king's public image might highlight **compassion**, behind the scenes, punishments for crimes or disloyalty could be severe. Nobles who conspired against the throne might be quietly executed or forced to commit suicide. Ordinary subjects heard rumors of secret trials, vanishings, and unexplained deaths. Such whispers kept people obedient. Everyone knew that the king held power not only from the gods but also from the threat of punishment.

7.3 Fear as a Tool of Governance

Even in the Middle Kingdom's more stable environment, the monarchy and local elites depended on **fear** to maintain order. Tax collectors toured the countryside, ensuring peasants handed over grain or livestock. If a district resisted, soldiers were dispatched to "encourage" compliance. Officials carried staffs or whips, sometimes depicted in tomb reliefs, signifying authority and willingness to use force.

To further solidify power, the state expanded the **bureaucracy**. Scribes tracked everything—harvest yields, labor assignments, and temple offerings. A single scribe's negative report could result in loss of land or property. People, especially peasants, feared the scribes as much as the king. In this environment, public gatherings might include announcements of criminals' punishments. The outcome—harsh sentencing—served as a warning to everyone, reminding them that laws were in place and would be strictly enforced.

7.4 The Emergence of the Coffin Texts

During the Middle Kingdom, funerary practices expanded beyond the elite class of pharaohs and top nobles. Previously, **Pyramid Texts** had been reserved for royalty, inscribed on tomb walls to protect the king in the afterlife. Now, **Coffin Texts** appeared. These were spells written on coffins that allowed a broader range of individuals—often officials, merchants, or lesser nobles—to guard themselves against afterlife dangers.

But this new accessibility also brought **fear**. If more people could harness powerful spells, what if they misused them? Some believed that unscrupulous priests or tomb artisans might sell these spells to criminals, enabling them to protect themselves from divine punishment. Stories spread of greedy officials who got hold of potent incantations, raising concerns that the very barriers meant to keep the afterlife orderly could be bypassed or corrupted.

7.5 The Rise in Tomb Robberies

One of the darkest aspects of Middle Kingdom society was the ongoing **tomb robbery** phenomenon. Despite the attempt to restore order, robberies increased—perhaps due to lingering poverty in certain regions or the lure of wealth placed with the dead. While the pharaoh and the upper class tried to fortify tombs with hidden chambers and false passages, grave looters grew bolder.

Legends describe entire crews of thieves who specialized in break-ins, moving at night with torches and metal tools. They sometimes bribed local guards or officials to turn a blind eye. Neighbors might hear muffled hammering under cover of darkness and suspect that a nearby tomb was being plundered. Some tomb owners (or their families) took extra steps, hiring private guards or leaving curses inscribed on doorways. That fear—of losing one's eternal rest or having a parent's tomb violated—added to the tension of daily life.

7.6 Security Measures and Guardian Statues

To combat robberies, tomb builders in the Middle Kingdom devised **guardian statues**—small or life-sized figures placed in passageways. These statues often wore fierce expressions or held weapons. Some had inscriptions threatening intruders with magical retaliation, such as blindness, madness, or disease. While we do not have direct evidence that these curses were always effective, the psychological impact was real.

Imagine a thief sneaking into a dimly lit corridor, only to come face-to-face with a statue carved to look like a snarling demon. Even if the thief did not believe in magic, the oppressive atmosphere could sow doubt. Many Egyptians firmly accepted that spirits and gods roamed the afterlife. Just the notion that a guardian statue might come alive and attack them could be enough to deter an inexperienced robber. Yet the truly determined criminals pressed on, driven by desperation or greed.

7.7 Priesthood Power Struggles and Dark Rituals

As the monarchy stabilized under Mentuhotep II and his successors, **priests** became powerful figures controlling temples, receiving tributes, and overseeing rituals. Temple treasuries swelled with donations from the king and wealthy patrons. This rise in wealth turned some priesthoods into political players, capable of challenging local governors or even the pharaoh himself.

Struggles emerged over how to interpret certain rituals, who had the right to perform them, and which gods deserved the most lavish offerings. Some priests dabbled in **secretive rites** that outsiders found frightening—animal sacrifices, complex incantations, or nighttime ceremonies to invoke protective deities. Ordinary Egyptians might see flickering lights and hear chanting from temple courtyards at midnight, fueling rumors that the priests were summoning spirits or punishing those who offended the gods.

In times of crisis—like drought or a plague—priests might accuse certain communities or individuals of angering the gods. Anyone labeled a heretic or blasphemer risked being cast out or worse. A sense of dread hung over religious life: while the temple could offer salvation and guidance, it could also demand strict obedience.

7.8 The Mummification Process Evolving

By the Middle Kingdom, **mummification** techniques had improved. Embalmers were more skilled at preserving bodies, removing organs through small incisions, and using natural salts and resins effectively. The goal was to keep the flesh intact for the afterlife. But the process was not pretty. It involved cutting into corpses, extracting intestines and other organs, and placing them into canopic jars guarded by deities like **Imsety**, **Hapi**, **Duamutef**, and **Qebehsenuef**.

Outsiders or lower-class Egyptians who had never seen the process up close might have found it gruesome, even terrifying. The strong smell of chemicals, the sight of embalmers handling cadavers, and the presence of sacred amulets brought to mind possible curses. Some believed that a vengeful spirit might linger around its own body, especially if the embalming was done poorly or if the correct prayers were missed. Fear of accidentally angering the deceased's spirit haunted those who worked as assistants in these workshops.

7.9 The Threat of Unhappy Ghosts

In the Middle Kingdom, the concept of the **restless dead** took on clearer shape. If a soul felt it had been wronged—either in how the body was handled or in how the family upheld funerary offerings—the spirit could return to haunt the living. Families who neglected to bring offerings to their relatives' tombs risked encountering angry ghosts in their dreams or experiencing unexplained misfortunes.

Petty disputes among families sometimes led to accusations that one side had "sent a ghost" to torment the other. Scribes recorded letters to the dead where the living would beg ancestors to stop afflicting them with sickness or unlucky events. This belief kept society cautious about funeral rites: no one wanted to risk an offended spirit. Everyone knew stories of apparitions trailing behind farmers in the fields or lurking at the edge of villages at dusk, demanding offerings or revenge.

7.10 The Role of Magical Texts in Everyday Life

While official religious practice took place in temples, **magic** pervaded daily life. Charm scrolls, amulets, and incantations were sold or shared among common people. Not all of these spells were for malevolent purposes; many protected against snakebites, scorpion stings, or diseases. But some individuals likely used magic to harm rivals, calling upon dark forces to bring curses or nightmares.

Fear of such sorcery fueled social suspicion. If a neighbor's child fell mysteriously ill, families might wonder if someone placed a hex on them. If a farmer's crops failed while his rival's flourished, could it be black magic? Accusations of sorcery sometimes led to violent confrontations or trials led by local priests. The combination of widespread belief in magical power and the sense that the afterlife was filled with volatile spirits created an undercurrent of dread in Middle Kingdom communities.

7.11 Environmental Concerns and Crop Failures

Despite the relative stability of the reunified Egypt, the **Nile floods** were not always predictable. Years of low inundation could lead to poor harvests, spiking grain prices. People remembered the horrific famines of the First Intermediate Period, so even a single year of subpar flooding could send waves of anxiety through the land. It took only a few rumors—reports of a dry year in Upper Egypt, for instance—to spark panic selling or hoarding of food.

Pharaohs tried to implement better irrigation and storage facilities. They also carried out grand religious ceremonies to appease the gods, particularly **Hapi**, the personification of the Nile flood. But if such measures failed, blame quickly fell on possible "sinners" or "cursed individuals." Some local officials spread the idea that the gods withheld water because certain districts harbored criminals, tomb raiders, or those disrespecting funerary customs. This environment of paranoia forced people to be vigilant about their own piety, lest they be accused of causing natural disasters.

7.12 Lore of the Labyrinth at Hawara

One of the most mysterious and, for some, frightening monuments of the Middle Kingdom is the so-called **Labyrinth** near Hawara, credited to **Amenemhat III**. This huge complex included many chambers, courtyards, and passages. Later writers described it as a place easy to get lost in, with complicated corridors and false doors. Though archaeologists debate its true layout, ancient Egyptians believed it housed secrets, treasures, or even hidden tombs.

Whispers suggested that the Labyrinth contained **traps** to catch unwary intruders—sliding slabs of stone or pits covered by flimsy boards. Others spoke of hidden chambers used for dark rituals, where priests might call upon underworld gods to protect the king's eternal rest. Parents might scare children into obedience by warning that if they wandered too far, the Labyrinth's curses would claim them. Whether or not these legends were factually correct, their persistence reveals a culture that found both wonder and terror in grand architectural feats.

7.13 "Letters to the Dead" and Fear of the Unseen

An intriguing practice that became more documented in the Middle Kingdom was writing **"Letters to the Dead."** Individuals penned messages on pottery shards or papyrus addressed to deceased relatives or friends, asking for help or forgiveness. Some letters pleaded for protection against enemies, health issues, or misfortune. In return, the living offered to keep providing offerings at the tomb.

Such letters reflect the Egyptian fear that the dead had **power** over the living, especially if they were neglected. They also show a desperate desire to influence the unseen world. If a ghost was tormenting someone, writing a letter could be a way to negotiate peace. Yet it was also risky—acknowledging a spirit's power might strengthen its claim. These letters represent a window into the Middle Kingdom mindset, where the boundary between life and death felt thin, and fear of the unknown shaped daily actions.

7.14 Popular Stories: Demons in the Dark

The Middle Kingdom saw a flourishing of **literature**, including tales and teachings. While many had moral or educational themes, some contained frightening elements—demons, shape-shifters, or enchanted creatures lurking in deserts or tombs. Stories like the "Tale of the Shipwrecked Sailor" hinted at supernatural islands, giant serpents, and the possibility of encountering otherworldly beings if one strayed from the Nile.

These stories, passed down orally and sometimes written on papyrus, served as warnings. Children learned not to wander alone at night or explore abandoned tombs. Adults were reminded that the desert was dangerous, filled with creatures both real and mythic. This emphasis on the supernatural fed into broader fears about curses, evil magic, and malevolent forces that might be unleashed if sacred boundaries were violated.

7.15 Curse Formulas: Protective or Threatening?

Curses were not unique to the Middle Kingdom, but the period saw more explicit **"curse formulas"** inscribed in tombs or on funerary objects. Simple statements like: "Whoever enters this tomb in an impure manner, the crocodile and hippopotamus shall devour him; the lion shall consume his bones." Such threats blended the power of real animals with spiritual doom.

While the purpose was to scare off tomb robbers, many Egyptians took these words seriously. Merely reading them out loud could cause anxiety, as if speaking the curse might activate it. Sometimes, travelers or laborers forced to work near old tomb sites worried that disturbing even a fallen stone might draw down the tomb-owner's wrath. Officials tried to assure them that official tasks were sanctioned by the gods, but fear of an unintentional curse lingered.

CHAPTER 8

Military Might in the Middle Kingdom and the Horrors of Warfare

While the Middle Kingdom offered internal unity, it also led to **expansion** beyond Egypt's traditional borders. Pharaohs aimed to secure valuable trade routes, control resources like gold and copper, and defend against threats real or imagined. This push for military might introduced new forms of fear—conscripted soldiers marched off to foreign lands, fortresses loomed at border regions, and entire populations faced brutal subjugation or heavy tribute. Warfare in the Middle Kingdom was not as grandly recorded as in later periods, but it carried its own horrors. From raids into Nubia to border conflicts in the Sinai, violence became a fact of life for many Egyptians.

8.1 The Middle Kingdom's Push into Nubia

One of the most significant military efforts of Middle Kingdom pharaohs was the **expansion into Nubia**, located to the south of Egypt. Nubia was rich in gold, ebony, and other resources. Under rulers like **Senusret III** and **Amenemhat III**, Egypt built a chain of forts along the Nile to secure these resources and keep control over local tribes.

For the Egyptians, Nubia was both an opportunity and a danger. Tribal groups in the region could raid Egyptian settlements if not contained. The fear of these Nubian warriors—reputed for their skill with bows—motivated the pharaohs to send expeditions that subdued or scattered local communities. Captured Nubians might be taken as slaves, forced to labor in quarries or farmland. For the Nubians, this was a time of despair as Egyptian forces destroyed villages and demanded loyalty, forever changing the cultural landscape of the region.

8.2 Building Fortresses and the Fear Factor

Along the southern border, imposing **fortresses** like **Semna**, **Kumma**, and others rose up. These were massive complexes with thick walls, towers, and barracks for Egyptian troops. Their presence was a message to locals: Egypt would crush any rebellion swiftly. The forts also became centers of tax collection, extracting wealth in the form of gold dust, cattle, or captives.

Life inside these fortresses was harsh. Soldiers faced scorching heat, isolation from their families, and the constant threat of surprise attacks by Nubian raiders. Commanders enforced discipline with strict punishments—whippings, imprisonment, or even summary executions for desertion. Meanwhile, Nubians living near the forts had to endure forced tribute and the fear that at any moment, a suspicious official could accuse them of treachery. These fortresses embodied Egypt's ambition and its willingness to use fear to maintain control.

8.3 Harsh Realities of Military Campaigns

When the king launched a campaign—whether to Nubia, Libya, or the Sinai—the army sometimes swelled with **conscripted peasants** who had no choice but to join. Local officials would announce that a new military push was under way; families had to provide able-bodied men. These recruits left their farms, uncertain of when or if they would return. Tales of brutal marches across deserts, battles against fierce enemies, and the possibility of dying far from home spread among the population.

Provisions were often scarce. Soldiers marched with basic rations of bread, onions, and water skins. If supplies ran out, they had to forage or seize food from local populations, fueling hatred and fear wherever they passed. Opponents, in turn, sometimes adopted guerrilla tactics—ambushing Egyptian columns at night, slaughtering stragglers, or poisoning wells. Letters and inscriptions from this era offer glimpses of the anxiety soldiers faced: thirst, disease, and the possibility of a terrifying death on distant soil.

8.4 The Power of the King: Amenemhat and Senusret

Pharaohs like **Amenemhat I** (founder of the 12th Dynasty) and **Senusret I** worked hard to display **military might** as part of their claim to legitimacy. They bragged about "smiting the enemies" of Egypt, a tradition dating back to the Early Dynastic Period. In reliefs and inscriptions, these kings appeared larger than life, wielding a mace or bow against foreign foes. The message was clear: the pharaoh was the guardian of order, defeating chaos personified by foreigners.

Yet behind these grand images lay the reality of forced labor, high taxes to fund campaigns, and propaganda that might have distorted actual events. Some victories could have been minor skirmishes portrayed as grand conquests. Still, the threat of the king's wrath felt real. Local governors, priests, and scribes repeated official accounts, ensuring the population believed in the king's supernatural ability to destroy enemies. Doubting the royal propaganda was dangerous and could brand one as disloyal.

8.5 War Trophies and Public Displays

Victorious generals or pharaohs sometimes brought back **trophies** from war—exotic animals, precious metals, or **captured foreign leaders**—to prove their success. These could be displayed in temple courtyards, turning the humiliation of enemies into a public spectacle. Sometimes, bound prisoners were paraded through towns, forced to kneel before the statue of the king, or even executed as part of a ritual sacrifice.

While these events boosted the pharaoh's prestige, they also sent a clear signal to Egyptians about the fate of traitors. Disloyalty was equated with foreignness, something outside the divine order. Anyone seen collaborating with "barbarians" risked facing the same humiliations. The fear of being labeled an enemy of the state, paraded in chains, or sacrificed before a crowd was strong motivation to remain obedient to the throne.

8.6 The Role of Fear in Maintaining the Border

Egypt's borders during the Middle Kingdom were not as secure as modern boundaries. Desert tribes, migrant groups, and foreign traders frequently crossed them. To maintain control, the pharaoh relied on intimidation. Soldiers stationed at border forts checked anyone trying to pass, demanding fees or tribute. Some caravans were detained if an officer suspected they might be carrying contraband or be allied with enemies.

Inscriptions at forts sometimes record harsh punishments for unauthorized crossing—hands cut off, forced labor, or death. The same fear that regulated internal taxes now extended to the frontiers. Travelers who had to journey for trade or personal reasons found themselves at the mercy of these fortress officials, who could accuse them of spying or smuggling. Many probably resorted to bribes, fueling corruption and reinforcing a climate where fear overshadowed trust.

8.7 Brutality Against Rebels

Whenever a **revolt** erupted—whether by disgruntled peasants, local nomarchs, or border populations—Egyptian rulers responded with brutal crackdowns. The Middle Kingdom inscriptions occasionally mention entire villages razed to the ground, fields burned, and water supplies destroyed to punish uprisings. Survivors could be taken as slaves or forcibly relocated to ensure they posed no further threat.

For the peasants caught in these rebellions, the terror was twofold: they feared the rebels might pillage their homes if they stayed loyal to the pharaoh, yet if they cooperated with the rebels, they faced the pharaoh's retaliation. Some individuals tried to flee, joining nomadic groups in the desert or seeking refuge in distant regions. Yet living outside the Nile Valley was itself perilous, with limited water and constant risk of bandit attacks.

8.8 Tools of War: Chariots and Bows

The Middle Kingdom saw improvements in **bows**, arrows, and the organization of infantry. The use of horses and **chariots** would become far more pronounced in later periods (notably the New Kingdom), but the seeds were planted here. Skilled archers could strike enemies at a distance, creating fear among those who had never faced such precise missile attacks.

Some Egyptians spoke in hushed tones about powerful "divine bows" crafted with magical spells so they never missed. Others worried about new metal weapons—bronze daggers, spears, and axes—that turned minor skirmishes into bloody slaughters. The king's workshops in Memphis or Thebes might produce these weapons in large quantities, distributing them to loyal garrisons. The presence of advanced weaponry increased the stakes of every conflict, making villages on the receiving end of a raid even more vulnerable.

8.9 The Horrors of Naval Warfare on the Nile

Many forget that the Nile itself was a battlefield. **Egyptian warships**, often simple wooden vessels with a complement of archers, could travel quickly along the river. They intercepted smugglers or attacked rebellious towns near the banks. A small fleet could arrive suddenly at dawn, unleashing volleys of arrows before landing troops.

Naval battles were chaotic. Soldiers boarded enemy boats, fighting hand to hand with spears and axes. If one vessel caught fire, the blaze could spread to others. Survivors jumped overboard, risking drowning or crocodile attacks. For towns along the Nile, the sight of warboats on the horizon signaled potential destruction. Rumors circulated of villagers dragged onto ships as prisoners, never to be seen again. This watery dimension of warfare added a new layer of dread for anyone who lived near the river.

8.10 The Fear of Enemy Gods

Egyptians believed strongly in their own pantheon, but they also recognized that other lands had gods, sometimes identified with Egyptian deities or seen as malevolent forces. Soldiers marched into foreign territories uncertain about the local gods' power. They might fear curses from these foreign divinities or worry that an angry local spirit could sabotage their campaigns.

In some inscriptions, kings boasted of smashing the foreign gods' images, "purifying" temples of defeated regions. But the common soldier might quietly wonder if destroying an enemy's shrine could invite spiritual vengeance. Tales of men who fell ill after desecrating a foreign statue circulated, reinforcing the notion that even in victory, one must be cautious. Fear was not only a weapon the Egyptians wielded; sometimes it haunted them, too.

8.11 Raids on Neighboring Territories

Beyond major campaigns, **raids** were frequent. Egyptian forces might strike a border zone for quick plunder—cattle, grain, or slaves—then retreat before a larger enemy force could respond. Conversely, tribes outside Egypt might attempt the same. These raids created a culture of **constant anxiety** for anyone living near the frontiers. One day's peaceful farming could turn into a nightmare if a band of raiders appeared.

Women and children were especially vulnerable—taken captive, sold into slavery, or left behind in burned-out settlements. In the aftermath of a raid, survivors might discover that grain stores were emptied and livestock stolen, condemning them to starvation if no relief came from the central government. The memory of these raids built a deep-seated fear that shaped local alliances, as villages banded together in hopes of fending off attackers.

8.12 Captives and Slavery in the Middle Kingdom

Slavery existed on a varying scale in Ancient Egypt. It was not always identical to later forms of chattel slavery, but **captives** from war or raids could become forced laborers in estates, temples, or royal projects. They might be branded or tattooed to show their status. Children of captives could grow up as domestic servants. Freed slaves were rare and often still tied to the land or institution that owned them.

This system thrived on fear. Captives who disobeyed or tried to escape risked beatings or death. Their owners used them for heavy labor, such as digging canals, quarrying stone, or building royal structures. Meanwhile, free peasants who saw how harshly slaves were treated might feel relief that they still had their freedom—but also a gnawing worry that if war came to their region, they could share the same fate.

8.13 Witchcraft Accusations in Wartime

In times of war, social panic intensified. The unexpected defeat of an Egyptian detachment or the sudden death of a high-ranking commander could be blamed on **witchcraft**. Soldiers might accuse local women of cursing the army. Entire villages could face reprisals if a priest declared that "dark magic" was behind the troops' misfortune. Houses were burned, and suspected witches executed without trial.

Such episodes show how deeply fear intertwined with warfare. People already worried about arrows and spears, but now they also had to guard against invisible "evil eyes." Commanders sometimes consulted temple oracles before marching, hoping to identify and punish any magical threats in advance. If an oracle named a suspect—rightly or wrongly—that individual was often doomed.

8.14 Soldiers' Accounts: Letters from the Front

Some papyrus fragments preserve **letters written by soldiers** to their families. These brief documents often mention hunger, disease, and the heartbreak of being separated from loved ones. One might read: "The water is foul, my rations are small, and the men are fearful of the enemy's night attacks." Another might speak of seeing fellow soldiers collapse from heat or dehydration in the desert.

The tone in these letters sometimes shows weariness and dread. The soldier begs his family to pray for him or make offerings to keep him safe from curses and foreign gods. In a society that prized bravery and loyalty, the very fact that soldiers expressed fear in writing is telling. It indicates that the mental burden of war weighed heavily on them, overshadowing the propaganda of glorious conquest.

8.15 The Aftermath of War: Broken Towns and Broken Spirits

When a Middle Kingdom campaign ended—whether successful or not—there were survivors who returned home forever changed. Some had witnessed or committed acts of violence that haunted their dreams. Villages that had been on the receiving end of Egyptian aggression often lay in ruins, their temples desecrated, and local gods dishonored. Crops were destroyed, leading to famine in regions that once prospered.

The official record might proclaim a great triumph, but individual stories told of lost limbs, orphaned children, and burned homes. Anxiety about the next campaign loomed. In many areas, local administrators tried to rebuild, extracting more taxes to cover the costs. This cycle of **war and recovery** left scars. People in border zones developed a deep-seated fear and resentment toward the central government. Some might have even welcomed future chaos if it meant escaping the tyranny of repeated invasions and forced labor.

CHAPTER 9

The New Kingdom's Valley of the Kings and Tomb Curses

The **New Kingdom** (c. 1550–1070 BCE) is the era of some of Egypt's most famous pharaohs, including Hatshepsut, Thutmose III, Akhenaten, and Ramses II. This period followed the Middle Kingdom and the chaotic Second Intermediate Period. It was a time when Egypt expanded its borders, established strong international trade, and built lavish monuments and temples. Yet, behind these glories lay a new focus on **hidden tombs**, **curses**, and unsettling beliefs about the afterlife. The Valley of the Kings is perhaps the most famous example—an isolated desert necropolis where pharaohs and some nobles were buried in rock-cut tombs to protect them from thieves and prying eyes. But the desire for secrecy and strong defenses also gave rise to tales of **dangerous curses** meant to strike down anyone who violated these sacred spaces.

9.1 A Shift in Burial Traditions

During the Old and Middle Kingdoms, massive pyramids and grand mastabas served as the main burial places for royalty. However, these structures made it easy for looters to target royal tombs. By the start of the New Kingdom, pharaohs began hiding their tombs in a remote valley on the west bank of the Nile across from Thebes (modern Luxor). This location became known as the **Valley of the Kings**.

The shift reflected a new approach: build elaborate tombs underground, conceal their entrances, and rely on a network of corridors and hidden rooms to deter grave robbers. The tombs included hidden passages, fake burial chambers, and complicated designs. Yet, as we will see, even these efforts often failed to keep thieves away. Fear of desecration did not stop criminals, but it fueled the creation of powerful curses and elaborate tomb defenses.

9.2 Choosing the Valley of the Kings

Why choose a barren desert valley? The area behind the cliffs of Deir el-Bahri and further west was remote and hard to reach. There was also a natural pyramid-shaped peak known as al-Qurn ("The Horn") overlooking the valley. Some Egyptians saw it as a symbol of the primeval mound or a sign of protective deities. The stark beauty and dryness of the desert may also have assisted in preserving the burial goods.

Yet, for workers who built these tombs, the place was **harsh**. They toiled in underground chambers, chiseling rock in dim torchlight, breathing in dust, and facing the very real risk of cave-ins or accidents. Some might have whispered of ghosts or spirits guarding the valley. Others believed that desert demons lurked in the canyons, waiting to pounce on anyone wandering alone after dark.

9.3 The Role of Deir el-Medina Workers

A special group of artisans, builders, and painters lived in a village now called **Deir el-Medina**, located not far from the Valley of the Kings. These skilled laborers were responsible for carving and decorating the tombs of the pharaohs and high officials. Their lives were somewhat better than those of common farmers, as they received regular food rations, housing, and certain privileges. But with that came great **secrecy** and intense supervision.

They were sworn to protect royal secrets. If a worker revealed the location of a tomb's entrance or the layout of the burial chambers, they could face severe punishments—beatings, imprisonment, or even death. Rumors circulated that the pharaoh's officials used spies among the workforce, encouraging them to report on any suspicious talk. This atmosphere of distrust and fear made it easier for the authorities to keep control, ensuring the tombs' details remained hidden from outsiders.

9.4 Design of Tombs: Labyrinths and False Passages

Unlike pyramids, which were mostly vertical or broad structures, the **New Kingdom tombs** in the valley were carved horizontally (though often sloping) into the cliffs. Each tomb typically had corridors leading deeper into the rock, sometimes twisting around corners or descending staircases. At the end lay the burial chamber, often richly decorated with spells from the **Book of the Dead**, **Book of Gates**, or the **Amduat**—texts describing the pharaoh's voyage in the underworld.

To deter robbers, architects sometimes added **false doors** or blocked passageways with massive stone slabs. Some tombs featured vertical shafts that dropped into hidden pits, a literal trap for thieves. Although these measures aimed to scare or ensnare intruders, the truth is that many tombs were **violated** despite the complexity. Some of the best-known tombs show signs of repeated break-ins. But this threat only spurred the living to craft even more threatening **curses**.

9.5 The Concept of Curses in the New Kingdom

Egyptian curses had existed in various forms before, but the **Valley of the Kings** period gave them special fame. Some curses warned that anyone who defiled the tomb would be seized by the guardians of the underworld, or that the intruder's family line would perish. Others named specific punishments—blinding, madness, or diseases that would consume the violator's body.

Certain tomb walls included images of vicious deities: serpents with multiple heads, creatures with knives in place of hands, or composite beasts that devoured hearts. These figures were more than artistic fantasies; they symbolized protective forces that guarded the royal afterlife. To an uneducated robber, these monstrous figures carved in flickering torchlight might have been terrifying. Coupled with the curses inscribed around them, it felt as though the tomb itself was alive with avenging spirits ready to pounce.

9.6 Hatshepsut and Her Mortuary Complex

One of the earliest significant pharaohs of the New Kingdom was **Hatshepsut**, a powerful female ruler who reigned during the 18th Dynasty (around 1479–1458 BCE). While she chose to place her mortuary temple at Deir el-Bahri (not exactly in the main Valley of the Kings), the concept of tomb secrecy and special protection carried on. The walls of her temple depict scenes honoring gods and legitimizing her rule.

Hatshepsut's actual burial was in the Valley of the Kings, in a tomb that was once believed to be lost. Over time, stories emerged about curses linked to her temple complex—particularly because it was so grand and unique. People believed that tampering with such a sacred site, dedicated to a rare female pharaoh, might provoke especially severe divine wrath. Though modern discoveries reveal that much of the complex was vandalized by her successor, Thutmose III, the local population might have blamed **ghostly retribution** or curses for the temple's damage.

9.7 Thutmose III: The Warrior Pharaoh's Tomb

Thutmose III, who followed Hatshepsut, was known for his military conquests and expansion of Egypt's empire. He also built an impressive tomb in the Valley of the Kings, KV34, famous for its unusual design and extensive decoration. The walls depict scenes from the Amduat—a text describing the sun god Ra's nightly journey through the underworld. Fearsome images of serpents spitting fire, lakes of flames, and demons with sharp blades fill the corridors.

For devout Egyptians, these images served a religious purpose, guiding Thutmose III in the afterlife. For potential tomb robbers, however, it was a **graphic warning**: disturb this tomb, and you face the guardians who dwell in these netherworld realms. In later centuries, travelers to the area described the tomb's artwork with trepidation, claiming that reading the spells aloud might awaken the guardians. Such beliefs contributed to the aura of dread around the entire valley.

9.8 Tomb Robbers and the Harsh Realities

Despite the elaborate protective measures, tomb robbery remained a real threat throughout the New Kingdom. In fact, we have papyrus records documenting official inquiries into tomb robberies. Thieves sometimes included **local villagers**, **temple workers**, or even **officials** who had insider knowledge. They would break seals, pry open sarcophagi, and strip mummies of their valuables—amulets, jewelry, or precious metals.

When caught, these robbers faced brutal punishments. Court documents speak of beatings with rods, the severing of hands, or impalement for the ringleaders. The fear of being discovered or betrayed by an accomplice must have been intense. Some thieves tried to justify their actions by claiming poverty or hunger. Others insisted that they were compelled by corrupt officials. Either way, the state used them as examples to scare anyone else who dared to violate the tombs.

9.9 The Mystery of KV5 and the Royal Children

One of the largest tombs in the Valley of the Kings, known as **KV5**, belonged to the sons of **Ramses II**. Ramses II (often called Ramses the Great) reigned for over sixty years and had many children. KV5 is a sprawling complex with numerous chambers, corridors, and side rooms. Excavations reveal that the tomb might have been expanded over time as more royal family members died.

Some legends claim that KV5 had **special curses** to protect the royal children. Rumors said that the ghosts of these princes, cut down early in life, would guard the corridors. People in later eras spoke of hearing childlike voices echoing in the darkness or seeing faint lights dance in the tomb's depths. While these stories likely sprang from local folklore, they highlight how **fear** and **mystery** made the Valley of the Kings an unsettling place, even centuries after these tombs were sealed.

9.10 Ramses II's Own Tomb

Ramses II constructed a grand tomb for himself, designated **KV7**. Over time, it suffered flooding and damage. Yet, some of its passages were once filled with protective spells and curses. Ramses II was known for his ego and the propaganda of his victories—like the Battle of Kadesh. So it is not surprising that he wanted his final resting place to stand as a fortress against time and thieves.

In reality, though, KV7 was eventually robbed, like many others. The pharaoh's mummy was moved more than once in ancient times, finally discovered in a royal cache. The repeated relocations of royal mummies suggest that even high priests recognized that grave robbers posed a constant threat. If curses and hidden passages could not keep thieves out, the only remaining option was to remove the mummy to a secret location. This ongoing battle between preservation and violation fueled the belief that powerful **magical retribution** existed for those who dared to loot.

9.11 The High Priests and the Reburial Program

Toward the end of the New Kingdom, especially during the reign of the 20th Dynasty (about 1189–1077 BCE), tomb robberies escalated. The economy was struggling, and political power was weakening. As a desperate measure, **high priests of Amun** began a systematic "reburial program," moving many royal mummies from their original tombs to secret caches at places like Deir el-Bahri. They hoped to save the bodies—and the precious funerary objects—from further plunder.

Such reburials took place at night, in secrecy, sometimes accompanied by chanting of protective spells. Workers carried the coffins through the desert under guard. If discovered by thieves, they risked losing everything. The hush-hush nature of these operations contributed to rumors that the priests might be performing **dark rituals** or forging alliances with hidden powers to keep the kings' spirits at peace. The possibility of the priests also stealing valuables along the way could not be ruled out, and this fueled further suspicion and fear.

9.12 The Discovery of King Tutankhamun's Tomb

Although **Tutankhamun** reigned during the 18th Dynasty (around 1332–1323 BCE), his tomb (KV62) remained hidden and mostly intact until its modern discovery in 1922. While we are not delving into modern times, it is worth noting that stories of a **"curse"** surrounding Tutankhamun became legendary. Ancient Egyptians certainly placed curses in tombs, and while Tutankhamun's curses were not explicitly found on the tomb walls, the concept of a "mummy's curse" fits well into the ancient mindset.

Tutankhamun's tomb was relatively small compared to those of more famous pharaohs. Yet it still contained an astonishing amount of wealth and artwork. In ancient times, thieves had briefly entered it but did not manage a full-scale looting. The unrobbed riches discovered much later reflect the fear that tomb builders instilled—**fear** that might have deterred or at least minimized the efforts of ancient robbers.

9.13 Everyday People and the Valley's Haunting Reputation

Local Egyptians who lived near Thebes or Deir el-Medina held conflicting views about the Valley of the Kings. On one hand, it was a place of great **sanctity**. The pharaohs, considered living gods, resided there after death. On the other hand, it was a **forbidden zone**. Guards patrolled the paths, punishing trespassers. People told ghost stories of wandering souls seeking revenge. Desert animals like jackals (associated with Anubis, the god of mummification) howled at night, adding to the eerie atmosphere.

For children growing up in Thebes, the valley was a place they might see from afar but were warned never to enter alone. Elders spoke of men who ventured inside the cliffs to find treasure, only to return cursed or never return at all. These warnings passed from generation to generation, reinforcing the notion that the pharaoh's resting place was guarded by powerful forces beyond mortal comprehension.

9.14 The Workers' Fear of Royal Punishment

Workers at Deir el-Medina occasionally went on **strike**—a rare event in ancient times—when they were not paid their rations. Documents show they marched to local temples to protest. Their knowledge of the tombs' secrets gave them leverage. Officials worried that if the workers became too desperate, they might **spill information** or commit robberies themselves.

But the workers also feared retribution from the pharaoh or his high officials. They knew the monarchy considered the sanctity of tombs paramount. If even a rumor spread that a worker had stolen a single piece of gold or revealed a tomb's layout, that person could vanish under suspicious circumstances. The tension between protecting tomb secrets and demanding fair treatment remained a delicate balance, maintained by the threat of harsh punishment.

9.15 Magical Texts in the Tombs

Over the New Kingdom, funerary texts grew more elaborate. The **Book of the Dead**, a collection of spells and instructions for navigating the afterlife, became more common. Additional texts like the **Book of Caverns** and **Book of the Earth** appeared, describing horrifying creatures, lakes of fire, and hidden caverns filled with serpents or demons. Tomb walls displayed these fearsome images to ensure the king (or high official) passed safely through the underworld.

But these images also served as a **deterrent**. If a robber managed to break into a tomb and saw walls covered with spells invoking serpents that spat poison, or gods who wielded knives against evildoers, that robber might think twice. In a deeply religious culture, the power of such spells was not just superstition—it was believed to be real. Even hardened thieves might hesitate, believing they could face curses not only in this life but also after death.

9.16 The Royal Necropolis' Guards and Execution Sites

The pharaoh's administration stationed **armed guards** at strategic points in the Valley of the Kings, especially near newly sealed tombs. These guards were responsible for challenging any unauthorized person. They set up small huts or lookout posts. Sometimes, they employed dogs to sniff out intruders. Punishments for trespassing varied, but in the worst cases—like an attempted break-in—a captured thief could be **executed on the spot** to make an example.

Some scholars suggest that certain open areas near the valley entrances may have been used as impromptu **execution sites**, though direct evidence is scarce. However, the mere rumor of a place where criminals were put to death contributed to the atmosphere of fear. Locals might hear screams at night or see buzzards circling in the morning, fueling tales of savage punishment ordered by the gods or the pharaoh's officials.

9.17 Natural Dangers in the Valley

Beyond human threats, the Valley of the Kings had **natural hazards**—scorching daytime heat, sudden flash floods after rare desert rains, and venomous creatures like scorpions and snakes. A person who ventured into the area without proper knowledge or supplies risked perishing from dehydration or a bite.

Some believed these natural dangers were the direct manifestation of tomb curses. If someone got stung by a scorpion near a hidden entrance, it was seen as a sign of the tomb's protective powers. Stories of sudden floods washing away entire camps reinforced the idea that the desert itself defended the royal dead. These beliefs blurred the line between ordinary environmental risks and supernatural vengeance.

9.18 The Decline of the New Kingdom and Valley Looting

As the New Kingdom neared its end (around 1070 BCE), Egypt's central authority weakened again. Economic troubles, foreign invasions, and internal power struggles plagued the land. The tombs in the valley—rich with gold and other valuables—became more tempting than ever. Even well-intentioned priests or officials struggled to maintain order, and some turned to tomb robbing themselves in desperate times.

Many tombs were **ransacked**, leaving mummies damaged and their contents scattered or stolen. The heartbreak for devout Egyptians was deep: not only was the pharaoh's spirit insulted, but every act of robbery risked unleashing curses that might befall the entire community. Despite these fears, scarcity and greed proved too strong. The final stages of the New Kingdom reveal a society anxious about losing its spiritual anchor as well as its physical treasures.

9.19 Legacy of the Valley of the Kings

Though most tombs in the Valley of the Kings were eventually looted in antiquity, their legacy endures. Ancient Egyptians believed wholeheartedly in the **power** of curses, the protective might of guardians, and the harsh punishments that awaited tomb violators. This conviction shaped how they designed their burial places, how they policed them, and how they perceived the afterlife.

The fear surrounding the valley resonated through centuries of Egyptian history. Even after the monarchy's decline, local inhabitants retained memories of a sacred necropolis protected by vengeful spirits. The rumored curses, swirling with images of monstrous underworld gods, stand as a testament to the potent mix of religion and terror that defined the New Kingdom approach to death.

CHAPTER 10

The Cult of Amun and Terrifying Religious Power

During the New Kingdom, one deity rose above all others in terms of wealth, influence, and sheer power: **Amun** (also spelled "Amen" or "Amon"). Centered at Karnak Temple in Thebes, the Cult of Amun became an institution so wealthy and formidable that even the pharaohs had to court its favor. This chapter looks at how **Amun** gained dominance, the frightening rites performed by his priests, the oracles that could topple kings, and the sense of dread that surrounded a priesthood capable of controlling both spiritual and earthly power. From secret inner sanctums to oracular judgments, the Cult of Amun exemplified the fusion of religion and fear that shaped the New Kingdom.

10.1 The Rise of Amun in Thebes

Amun was not always the chief god of Egypt. Before the Middle Kingdom, he was a local Theban deity. But when Thebes emerged as a major power, first reuniting Egypt in the Middle Kingdom and again expelling the Hyksos in the early New Kingdom, its patron god soared in prominence. **Pharaohs** like Ahmose and Amenhotep I credited Amun for their military victories and showered his temple with riches.

By the time of **Hatshepsut** and **Thutmose III**, Karnak Temple had become a massive complex. Pharaohs added grand pylons, obelisks, and sanctuaries. Each construction project recognized Amun's role in granting the king success, from conquering Nubia to controlling trade routes. This success fed more donations and tributes into Amun's coffers, giving priests enormous wealth. They owned farmland, cattle, and workers—making the cult a powerhouse that sometimes rivaled the throne itself.

10.2 Temples as Centers of Wealth and Power

Unlike simple shrines, major **Amun temples** like Karnak and Luxor were sprawling city-like complexes. They had storerooms brimming with grain, precious metals, and imported goods. Workshops produced statues, amulets, and ritual items. Scribes recorded every donation, from gold ingots to herds of livestock. Pilgrims came from all over Egypt (and beyond) to present offerings or seek the god's favor.

This accumulation of resources allowed the priests to become influential in political affairs. In some cases, high priests of Amun negotiated directly with foreign powers or commanded armed guards. They could direct where temple wealth was spent: perhaps to repair city walls, support an expedition, or sponsor a festival. Pharaohs, seeking to maintain good relations, often granted these priests further privileges. Yet beneath the surface, the question remained: **Who truly held the power—king or god?** And if a pharaoh displeased the priesthood, what terrible fates might befall him?

10.3 The Oracle Phenomenon

One of the most **fearsome** aspects of Amun's cult was the use of **oracles**. Priests believed (or claimed) that the statue of Amun could communicate the god's will by nodding or moving in answer to a question. In practice, several priests likely maneuvered the statue behind a screen or used hidden means to make it sway. Nonetheless, the public perceived these movements as Amun speaking directly.

These oracles were used to settle disputes, confirm the legitimacy of a pharaoh, or condemn suspected criminals. If the oracle pointed to a man as a traitor, it could mean immediate imprisonment or execution. The accused had little hope of appeal because Amun's word was final. This gave priests enormous leverage. They could declare an individual guilty of conspiracy or bless a favored candidate for office. Many Egyptians trembled at the idea that a hidden group of priests could control Amun's "answers," shaping life and death with divine authority.

10.4 The Hidden Sanctuaries and Secret Rites

Temples like **Karnak** included restricted areas where only the highest-ranking priests and the pharaoh were allowed. One such area was the **Holy of Holies**, a dimly lit chamber holding the god's statue or sacred barque. Rituals there were conducted in strict secrecy. Witnessing them without permission was considered a grave offense.

Stories abounded of bizarre ceremonies, including the possible use of **blood** from animal sacrifices, chanting in unknown tongues, or the presence of masked priests embodying deities. While some of these tales might be exaggerated, they fed the public imagination. People believed that if the priests of Amun wanted to place a curse on someone—or even on a region—such secret rites could unleash divine wrath. The temple's thick walls concealed these rites, making them all the more mysterious and fearsome.

10.5 Festivals Displaying Amun's Might

On special occasions, the priests brought Amun's statue out of the Holy of Holies to join grand festivals, such as the **Opet Festival** in Thebes. The statue was carried on a barque adorned with gold and precious stones. Musicians, dancers, and soldiers paraded through the streets. While the festival appeared joyful, there was also an undercurrent of awe. People knew the statue represented Amun's living presence on Earth.

During these processions, oracles might be performed publicly. If someone asked whether the pharaoh had the support of Amun, the statue might tilt forward in agreement. Cheers rose from the crowd. But if the statue turned away or remained still, it signaled danger—a possible sign that the king had lost favor. The crowd might tremble, remembering stories of past rulers who fell from power after Amun withdrew his blessing. This public demonstration of the god's will reinforced the **fear** that a single unfavorable sign from Amun could condemn even a mighty pharaoh.

10.6 Threats to Pharaoh's Authority

While the pharaoh was traditionally the high priest of every deity, in the New Kingdom the **high priests of Amun** built their own power base. They ran estates, commanded workers, and maintained private militias. Over time, certain pharaohs found themselves competing with these priests for influence. Even a strong ruler like Thutmose III had to shower Karnak with gifts to keep the priesthood loyal.

A pharaoh who crossed Amun's cult might discover that oracles began to disfavor his decrees. Priests could claim a new "chosen one" should sit on the throne. This scenario fed paranoia in the royal court. Officials might spy for the priesthood, alerting them to any sign of the king's impiety. Rumors circulated of silent vendettas or curses placed upon disobedient monarchs. For example, if the Nile's floods were poor, the priesthood could subtly hint that the pharaoh had angered Amun. The fear of losing both spiritual and political legitimacy made many kings walk a fine line with the priests.

10.7 Dangers of Heresy: The Memory of Akhenaten

A major event in the 18th Dynasty was the **religious revolution** of **Akhenaten** (formerly Amenhotep IV), who tried to replace the worship of Amun (and other gods) with that of the Aten, a sun disk deity. Akhenaten closed Amun's temples, seized temple wealth, and moved the capital to a new city, Akhetaten (modern Amarna).

Though Akhenaten's reign does not fully belong to the mainstream cult of Amun, its aftermath terrified future pharaohs. After his death, the high priests of Amun led a backlash. They destroyed Akhenaten's statues and reopened Karnak, reinstating Amun's supremacy. In later generations, Akhenaten was labeled a **heretic**. Egyptians whispered stories of how he was punished in the afterlife, how his attempts at suppressing Amun led to famine or foreign invasions. This cautionary tale hung over all future rulers, reminding them of the fearsome consequences of defying the Cult of Amun.

10.8 Horemheb and the Restoration of Amun's Order

General **Horemheb** eventually took the throne after Tutankhamun and Ay, working closely with the Amun priesthood to erase the memory of Akhenaten. Horemheb launched punishments against officials who had supported Atenism, redistributing temple lands back to Amun. Inscriptions declared him as the champion of the old gods, an agent of restoration who reclaimed Egypt from heresy.

However, the priesthood's role in guiding—or coercing—Horemheb's policies was not overlooked. People understood that Horemheb needed the priests' support to stabilize the kingdom. The aura of fear that surrounded the Cult of Amun now extended beyond the temples; any official suspected of lingering loyalty to Atenism risked arrest or worse. Horemheb's rule showed that while the monarchy tried to appear in control, it shared power with a religious machine that had grown extremely strong.

10.9 Ramses the Great and the Glory of Amun

Ramses II (Ramses the Great) further strengthened Amun's cult. He built or expanded temples dedicated to the god across Egypt, from Abu Simbel in Nubia to the Ramesseum in Thebes. Official propaganda depicted Amun granting Ramses unlimited victories. In return, the pharaoh showered the temple with spoils of war. This mutual reinforcement created a cycle: the more conquests the pharaoh claimed, the richer Amun's temple became, and the more the priests declared him favored by the gods.

Yet behind the scenes, tension lurked. If Ramses ever lost a major battle or faced a crisis—like plague or famine—the people might interpret it as Amun's disfavor. In a kingdom steeped in superstition, the priests could subtly undermine the pharaoh by attributing disasters to a break with piety. Over time, this threat gnawed at the monarchy's sense of absolute power.

10.10 Ancient "Spiritual Terror": Temple Curses and Protective Magic

Amun's temples became known for **magical wards**—spells or inscriptions on temple walls claiming that those who harmed or defiled the sacred precinct would be struck by the **wrath of the god**. Some curses promised disfigurement, disease, or the total destruction of one's lineage. Priests recited these spells regularly, reinforcing the idea that the temple grounds were dangerous to trespassers.

Additionally, priests performed exorcisms and protective rites for those who could pay. This gave them further control. Wealthy Egyptians or officials might seek the temple's help to remove a curse or placate an angry spirit. If the priesthood decided not to cooperate—perhaps because the person had angered them—fear of supernatural punishment could isolate the individual socially. The temple's grip on magic and curses went far beyond the boundaries of Karnak; it extended into daily life, overshadowing business deals, marriages, and even petty disputes.

10.11 Oracular Decrees Against Enemies

Because oracles held such authority, the priests of Amun used them not just for spiritual guidance but also for political maneuvering. They could pronounce **oracular decrees** that condemned a rival official or forced the redistribution of lands. For commoners, hearing about these divine pronouncements was a sobering reminder of who truly ruled Egypt. Even the pharaoh depended on Amun's nod.

Stories circulated of individuals who tried to bribe priests to gain a favorable oracle. If caught, both parties might be punished. Yet, the possibility of using the god's "word" to ruin one's enemies tempted many. Fear of being falsely accused in an oracular session was real. People might avoid public gatherings in case a priest singled them out. In a land where the god "spoke" through men, no one felt entirely safe.

10.12 The Height of Priesthood Control: High Priests as Rulers

In the late New Kingdom, particularly under the **20th Dynasty** and the early Third Intermediate Period, high priests of Amun in Thebes held so much power that they effectively ruled Upper Egypt. While a pharaoh might still reign nominally from the north (in Tanis or Pi-Ramesses), the south obeyed the high priest. This scenario created a divided land: the pharaoh in the Delta, the priesthood in Thebes.

This division spelled out the ultimate **terror**: if you were a citizen in Thebes, you might answer directly to the priestly bureaucracy, which could impose taxes, muster troops, or enact harsh penalties. Some priests even minted their own local currency and placed their names on monuments—a kingly prerogative. For many Egyptians, it seemed as if Amun's priesthood had become a second royal court, one with the advantage of divine endorsement. Fear of angering the priests overshadowed daily life, for they possessed not only spiritual might but also political and military power.

10.13 Secret Police and Temple Guards

With great wealth and property under temple control, the priests maintained their own force of **temple guards**. Official documents mention these guards seizing suspected thieves or harassing travelers who lacked proper permission. If the temple's scribes suspected someone of stealing from the granaries or forging oracular decrees, the guards could make swift arrests, sometimes bypassing royal courts.

Moreover, rumors of a **secret police**—temple agents who blended into the community—spread among the populace. These undercover watchers might report seditious talk, such as complaints about high temple taxes or doubts about Amun's favor. People learned to remain quiet or speak in hushed tones. An unguarded remark about the priests' corruption or a joke about the god's statue could result in a nighttime arrest. This climate of suspicion fed an ever-present sense of dread.

10.14 Festival Blood Sacrifices

Although large-scale human sacrifice was not a mainstay of Egyptian religion, **animal sacrifices** were common, especially at big festivals. Bulls, rams, geese, and other creatures were slain in Amun's honor. Some foreign prisoners captured in warfare might also face ritual executions tied to festival celebrations. The public nature of these acts—blood spilling on altars while priests chanted spells—was meant to display the god's power over life and death.

For children and sensitive onlookers, these bloody rites could be terrifying. The bellowing of the animals, the smell of fresh blood in the sun, and the rhythmic chanting created an atmosphere of raw power. Priests insisted that these sacrifices maintained **maat** (divine order), providing spiritual energy for the god. But beneath the theological justifications lay the stark reminder: those who opposed Amun (or the priesthood) might find themselves on the receiving end of the blade.

10.15 The Burden of Donations and Tithes

Amun's growing dominance meant more and more resources were funneled into his cult. Pharaohs ordered entire populations to pay tithes—like a set percentage of their harvest—to Karnak or other Amun temples. Nomarchs and local officials also gave gifts to the temple to prove their loyalty. Over time, the priests accumulated so much land and wealth that their estates rivaled the royal treasury.

For everyday farmers and artisans, these demands were burdensome. During lean years, paying the temple's share could mean the difference between feeding a family or going hungry. Failing to pay invited accusations of impiety. The priests could claim that such disobedience angered Amun, potentially causing low Nile floods or plague. The fear of divine punishment—and the temple's tangible power—drove people to comply, even at great personal cost.

10.16 Political Intrigue and Priest-King Rivalries

In the final decades of the New Kingdom, tension grew between the monarchy and the priesthood. The high priests, such as Herihor and later successors, started taking on more titles and power. Some declared themselves "ruler of Thebes" or used phrases suggesting royal authority. While the pharaoh tried to maintain an image of unity, the country was effectively **split** between the northern king and the southern priests.

Political plots unfolded in the shadows. Royal messengers to Thebes sometimes vanished or returned with cryptic messages. Was the high priest planning a coup? Did the local army owe allegiance to the priesthood or the pharaoh? The entire situation brimmed with unspoken threats. Rumors of curses or hush-hush executions circulated in taverns and marketplaces. Egyptians who remembered the stable days of earlier New Kingdom pharaohs grew anxious, fearing a new wave of internal strife reminiscent of past intermediate periods.

10.17 Temple Treasures and Secret Storehouses

Amun's temple complexes, especially at Karnak, had **vast storehouses** filled with precious metals, carved statues, incense, and exotic imports from Nubia, Punt, or beyond. High priests and chief treasurers guarded these storehouses with elaborate locks and sealed doors. Only a handful of trusted individuals had permission to enter.

Because the exact inventory was known only to certain scribes, rumors ran wild about **hidden vaults** containing cursed objects or powerful magical relics. Some said that a single gem from these vaults, if stolen, would invoke Amun's fury on the thief's entire village. Others claimed the priests employed sorcerers to ensure that any stolen item would "call out" to its rightful owner until retrieved. These claims boosted the sense that the temple's wealth was protected not just by walls and guards, but by a supernatural force ready to punish transgressions.

10.18 Oracles in Warfare and Foreign Diplomacy

When the pharaoh planned a military campaign, it became customary to consult Amun's oracle. The statue was brought out, and the priests asked if the god approved. A favorable nod could rally troops and encourage allies. A negative response might halt the entire venture. Foreign diplomats, too, recognized the role of the Amun priesthood. Some came bearing lavish gifts, hoping to secure the temple's blessing or at least neutrality.

This gave the priests a **major role** in shaping foreign policy. If they disliked a certain alliance or had reason to fear a king's ambitions, they might sway the oracle against him. In effect, the priests could sabotage the king's war plans or push him into conflicts he otherwise would avoid. Soldiers grumbled about risking their lives for the temple's gain, but open criticism was rare—no one wanted to be labeled a heretic and face divine wrath.

10.19 Final Years of the New Kingdom: Religious Fear and Fragmentation

As the 20th Dynasty ended, pharaohs like Ramses XI struggled to hold the realm together. The high priest of Amun, a man named **Herihor** in Thebes, took on more royal titles, while another figure, Smendes, ruled in the north. Egypt was once again fracturing into regional powers. For ordinary people, this meant confusion about loyalty: should they pay taxes to the priest-king in Thebes or the pharaoh in Tanis?

Civil strife loomed, and the fear of divine punishment hung over every decision. Each side claimed Amun's favor. Oracles from Thebes might declare the northern government illegitimate, while local oracles up north might do the opposite. To the population caught in this spiritual tug-of-war, the dread of incurring the god's anger was constant. The lines between religious devotion and political manipulation became thoroughly entangled, culminating in the downfall of the New Kingdom and ushering in the Third Intermediate Period (c. 1070–664 BCE).

CHAPTER 11

The Reign of Hatshepsut and Unknown Threats

After the New Kingdom's early rulers stabilized Egypt and the Theban god Amun grew in power, a remarkable event happened in the 18th Dynasty: **a female pharaoh took the throne** and ruled with impressive authority for over two decades. Her name was **Hatshepsut** (c. 1479-1458 BCE). While history often remembers her for successful trade expeditions, beautiful temples, and internal peace, her reign also carried an undercurrent of fear and uncertainty. She was surrounded by unknown threats—including potential usurpers, uneasy nobles, and mysterious omens—and she fortified her legitimacy with religious propaganda that some regarded as frightening. In this chapter, we will explore the **darker and lesser-discussed aspects** of Hatshepsut's rule, including conspiracies, secretive measures to secure power, eerie temple activities, and the psychological tension of being a female king in a male-dominated society.

11.1 Hatshepsut's Path to Power: A Controversial Step

Hatshepsut was a daughter of King Thutmose I and became the principal wife (Great Royal Wife) of her half-brother, Thutmose II. When Thutmose II died young, he left an infant heir—**Thutmose III**—who was too young to govern. Hatshepsut took the role of regent, guiding the affairs of the kingdom until the child-king could rule. However, at some point early in her regency, Hatshepsut declared herself **"King of Upper and Lower Egypt."**

It was highly unusual, even shocking, for a woman to assume the full titles and regalia of a pharaoh. Ancient Egyptians believed in cosmic order (Maat), part of which was the notion that a male king represented Horus on Earth. By claiming this role, Hatshepsut defied centuries of tradition, which likely triggered **whispers of discontent** and fear among the elite. Some might have worried that the gods would punish Egypt for placing a woman on the throne. This anxiety could lead to conspiracies, silent or otherwise, to remove Hatshepsut and place Thutmose III in uncontested power.

11.2 Male Imagery and Fear of the Gods' Wrath

Early depictions of Hatshepsut showed her in female attire, but over time, she adopted traditional pharaonic symbols: the false beard, the kilt, and even a masculine body shape in statues. This transformation was not done lightly. She understood that the Egyptian mindset might interpret a female pharaoh as **anger toward the gods**—a break in divine order. To avoid frightening the populace with an "unnatural" sight, Hatshepsut's sculptors carefully reworked her images to appear more male.

Yet, these changes also carried a sense of **mystique**. Local priests and commoners wondered if Hatshepsut had made some secret pact with the gods, especially Amun, to legitimize her claim. Some records indicate that her advisors spread the story that Amun himself had fathered her, thus making her divine. This was not an uncommon claim for Egyptian kings, but in Hatshepsut's case, it was especially important to quell fears of divine disapproval. However, not everyone was convinced. The tension between public acceptance and private skepticism remained, prompting Hatshepsut to keep tight control over her court.

11.3 The Military and the Unknown: Threats from Within

Hatshepsut's main competitor for direct power was her stepson, **Thutmose III**, who technically was the rightful male heir. Initially a child, he posed no immediate threat. But as he grew older, many nobles and military commanders recognized he had a strong claim. Some might have considered removing Hatshepsut. It's unclear if any active revolt took place; official records remain silent. Yet the **absence** of evidence can sometimes speak volumes in ancient history. Hatshepsut or her loyal officials might have suppressed documents or put down small conspiracies quietly.

This undercurrent of potential **palace intrigue** kept Hatshepsut vigilant. She rewarded the army generously, aware they could quickly turn on her if commanded by a discontented faction. Meanwhile, Thutmose III was given positions in the military—possibly to occupy him or keep an eye on him—but he lacked real power while Hatshepsut was alive. For a female king, balancing power and fear was an art: too lenient, and conspiracies could grow; too harsh, and she might spark open rebellion. The fine line she walked was itself a source of dread in the palace halls.

11.4 The Grand Mortuary Temple at Deir el-Bahri: A Site of Mystery

Hatshepsut's most famous architectural achievement is her mortuary temple at **Deir el-Bahri**, nestled against towering cliffs on the west bank of the Nile, near the Valley of the Kings. This temple, known in ancient times as the "Djeser-Djeseru" ("Holy of Holies"), had a unique terraced design. Its elegant ramps and colonnades were striking, but there was also a sense of **otherworldly** aura. The imposing cliffs formed a natural amphitheater, and some Egyptians whispered that spirits or desert demons resided in the high rock faces.

At the temple, Hatshepsut had scenes carved to depict her divine birth—Amun visiting her mother in human form—validating her claim to rule. Some found this concept awe-inspiring, while others might have viewed it as blasphemous or a trick. The temple also featured chapels dedicated to the funerary cult and certain gods, including Hathor. **Secret rituals** might have been performed there at night—offerings to the gods, incantations for protecting Hatshepsut's spirit after death, and wards against enemies who would deface her memory. Locals sometimes spread rumors of **shadowy figures** moving through the colonnades under moonlight, fueling a sense of dread about what truly happened within those walls.

11.5 Journey to the Land of Punt: Eerie Tales of the Unknown

Another highlight of Hatshepsut's reign was her **expedition to Punt**, a land often associated with incense, myrrh trees, gold, and exotic products. Egyptians revered Punt as almost mythical, a place of divine scents. Hatshepsut famously depicted this journey on the walls of her Deir el-Bahri temple, celebrating a successful trade mission. While modern scholars believe Punt likely lay somewhere along the Red Sea coast or in the Horn of Africa, ancient Egyptians might have seen it as a mysterious realm filled with unknown **spirits** and **strange creatures**.

Stories told of monstrous beasts lurking in the dense forests or swamps near Punt. Sailors on Hatshepsut's ships might have feared storms at sea or encountering diseases foreign to Egypt. Some texts mention large birds, unusual fish, or venomous serpents not found along the Nile. Though the official record shows the expedition as a triumph, the actual journey must have been terrifying for participants—**voyaging beyond familiar lands** with only the pharaoh's blessing to shield them from both human and supernatural threats. The success of the mission reinforced Hatshepsut's image as favored by the gods, further deterring anyone who doubted her legitimacy. After all, a king who could safely travel to a potentially haunted region and return with riches surely enjoyed powerful divine protection.

11.6 Fear of the Afterlife: Ensuring Hatshepsut's Eternal Security

Like all pharaohs, Hatshepsut was deeply concerned about her afterlife. She believed that if her body was not preserved or if her tomb was disturbed, she would suffer eternal unrest. Her choice to build a tomb in the Valley of the Kings—and a separate mortuary temple—suggests she wanted security. The temple's walls included spells, praising her deeds and threatening dire consequences for those who might defile her memory. Egyptians believed that tomb curses were especially potent if a king or high priest invoked them.

The exact curses inscribed on Hatshepsut's monuments might not be as explicit as later tomb texts, but the **implication** was there: harming her tomb or erasing her name could bring retribution from the gods. This fearsome prospect extended to her enemies. They must have realized that if they destroyed her statues or defaced her inscriptions while she was alive, they risked incurring a divine penalty that could haunt them in this life and the next. Of course, ironically, after Hatshepsut's death, Thutmose III did remove many of her images—a testament to their ongoing power struggle. If curses existed, perhaps Thutmose III believed he could rely on his own divine authority to offset them.

11.7 Court Intrigues, Spies, and the "Unknown Threats"

While Hatshepsut's reign was relatively stable on the surface, hints of **court intrigue** appear in scattered records. Advisors like **Senenmut**, a commoner who rose to great power under Hatshepsut, attracted rumors. Some believed Senenmut and Hatshepsut had a personal relationship—an idea scandalous enough to spark talk of conspiracies. Others resented Senenmut for amassing wealth and building multiple tombs for himself.

Fear in the royal court manifested as hush-hush conversations, coded messages, and possible use of **spies** to track subversive talk. Priests of Amun generally supported Hatshepsut because she lavished the temple with donations. But any sign that they might shift loyalty to Thutmose III could unravel her authority. The question of how many people secretly desired a male king overshadowed everyday life in the palace. Hatshepsut likely placed trusted officials in key positions to root out plots before they gained traction. While no dramatic palace coup is recorded, the atmosphere of suspicion was real—**unknown threats** lurking in corners, waiting for a chance to strike.

11.8 Religious Propaganda: Terrifying Claims of Divine Will

To reinforce her position, Hatshepsut's scribes and priests spread the idea that **Amun** had specifically chosen her to rule. Some temple reliefs show her in direct contact with Amun, receiving the ankh (symbol of life) from him. In a deeply religious culture, this was a potent message: resisting Hatshepsut meant resisting the will of the supreme god.

From a negative perspective, this propaganda could be frightening for commoners and nobles alike. If they dared to speak against the female king, they might be labeled **blasphemers** and face both earthly punishment and divine wrath. Additionally, local oracles might have been manipulated to confirm Hatshepsut's legitimacy, further intimidating her critics. In effect, she weaponized religion to keep any dissent at bay.

11.9 Death and the Mysterious End of Hatshepsut

Hatshepsut died around 1458 BCE under circumstances not fully known. Some scholars suggest she died of natural causes; others suspect a more sinister end, though no conclusive evidence exists. If there was foul play, it could have been orchestrated by factions loyal to Thutmose III or by resentful courtiers. The lack of detailed records raises the possibility of a carefully covered-up plot.

Whatever the cause, once Hatshepsut was gone, Thutmose III took full power. Later in his reign, he had many of her statues and inscriptions defaced or removed. This act, sometimes referred to as a **damnatio memoriae**, was a form of posthumous vengeance—erasing Hatshepsut's name from history, thereby denying her presence in the afterlife (according to Egyptian belief). The fear that one could be "killed" again in the next world by having one's name destroyed was a chilling reality in ancient Egypt. It shows how the terror extended beyond physical life into the spiritual realm.

11.10 The Legacy of Hatshepsut's Fearful Reign

Despite the negativity cast on her memory, Hatshepsut likely left behind a legacy of more stable trade, architectural achievement, and internal peace. Yet beneath these successes lay the **constant dread** of a regime that had to justify itself in the face of tradition. Whether it was forging a divine lineage to stave off rumors of the gods' wrath or maintaining secret watchers in the court, Hatshepsut's reign was a delicate dance with fear.

This story reveals that even in an age of monumental temples and relative prosperity, the monarchy had to navigate hidden currents of conspiracy, religious intimidation, and personal anxiety. Hatshepsut's example proved that a determined leader—woman or man—could hold power as long as they managed these fears effectively. But once they slipped, the old order could quickly reassert itself, destroying reputations and rewriting history. In the next chapter, we will see how another pharaoh, **Akhenaten**, took an even more extreme religious path, causing a different kind of terror among the population as he challenged the centuries-long worship of Amun and the other gods.

CHAPTER 12

Akhenaten's Religious Shift and Dread Among the Masses

While Hatshepsut had expanded Amun's dominance to legitimize her rule, a later pharaoh of the 18th Dynasty attempted the opposite—he tried to **overthrow** Amun's cult altogether. His name was **Akhenaten** (originally Amenhotep IV), and he became one of history's most controversial rulers. Akhenaten's radical push for **monotheistic** worship of the **Aten** (the sun disk) shocked the nation, displacing centuries of tradition. This upheaval caused widespread fear: priests and commoners worried about divine retribution, soldiers and bureaucrats feared losing their status, and the social order teetered on the brink. In this chapter, we will examine how Akhenaten's revolution began, the terror it provoked, and the ultimate backlash that followed his death.

12.1 Amenhotep IV Becomes Akhenaten: The Early Signs of Trouble

Before his name change, Akhenaten was known as Amenhotep IV, the son of **Amenhotep III** and Queen Tiye. The name Amenhotep means "Amun is satisfied," reflecting a royal lineage deeply tied to the Cult of Amun. Initially, Amenhotep IV showed reverence for Amun, but something shifted in his early reign. Texts and reliefs suggest he began favoring a lesser-known aspect of the sun god, the **Aten**—depicted simply as a solar disk with rays ending in hands.

At first, this preference might have seemed like typical syncretism. Egyptian religion often merged deities or emphasized certain gods at different times. But quickly, Amenhotep IV's devotion to the Aten grew forceful. He built a temple to the Aten near the major complex at Karnak, overshadowing existing shrines to Amun. Priests of Amun watched nervously. Rumors circulated that the king was drifting into heresy. The abruptness of these changes spurred anxiety about what might happen if Amun's wrath descended on Egypt.

12.2 Declaring War on the Old Gods

Around the fifth year of his reign, Amenhotep IV took a drastic step: he **changed his name** to **Akhenaten**, meaning "Beneficial to the Aten," and soon declared that the Aten was the **only** true god. This was an unprecedented move in a polytheistic land. Akhenaten closed Amun's temples, confiscated their wealth, and removed references to other gods from monuments. In effect, he set out to **erase** the old pantheon.

For the general populace, this was a **nightmare** scenario. Since the Old Kingdom, Egyptians had prayed to multiple gods—Amun, Ra, Osiris, Isis, Hathor, Ptah, and many others. They believed these deities oversaw every aspect of life: the Nile's flood, fertility of crops, childbirth, and passage to the afterlife. Now, the king was ordering them to abandon these protective forces and worship only the Aten. Priests from other temples faced sudden unemployment. Entire religious festivals were banned. Fear spread that the old gods would retaliate with **famine, disease, or invasion** if spurned.

12.3 Building Akhetaten (Amarna): A Capital of Isolation

To further distance himself from the old religious centers (like Thebes), Akhenaten built a new capital city called **Akhetaten** (modern **Amarna**), located in Middle Egypt on a stretch of desert plain. He boasted that the city's boundaries were chosen by the Aten, free from the shadow of Amun's temples. Huge stone boundary stelae were cut in the surrounding cliffs, declaring the city sacred to the Aten.

Workers rushed to construct temples, palaces, and noble houses. The temples dedicated to the Aten had **open-air courtyards**, allowing sunlight to flow in—unlike traditional enclosed sanctuaries for other gods. This design symbolized the Aten's direct presence. But for many Egyptians, the city felt **desolate**. Legend says that the wind howled across the barren plain at night, stirring up swirling sands. Soldiers and bureaucrats forced to relocate left behind families, property, and the comforting presence of their traditional gods. Some whispered that this entire city was a **trap**, a place where the king's madness would lead them all to ruin.

12.4 Radical Art and Strange Depictions of the Royal Family

Under Akhenaten, artistic style changed dramatically. Traditional Egyptian art followed rigid conventions, but now, reliefs showed the royal family with elongated limbs, swollen bellies, narrow chests, and alien-looking faces. Akhenaten and his chief wife, **Nefertiti**, were depicted in intimate family scenes, kissing their children under the rays of the Aten. Some images showed the Aten's rays ending in tiny hands holding the **ankh** (symbol of life) to the royal nostrils.

To the uninitiated, these depictions were **unsettling**. Conspiracy theories might have spread that the royal family was physically transforming due to the Aten's power. Rumors of curses on those who mocked their appearance also circulated. The common folk found it **eerie** that the king refused to uphold the old gods' traditions while adopting bizarre new imagery. Anxiety grew that something unnatural was happening at the heart of Egyptian leadership.

12.5 Persecution of Old Beliefs and Forced Conversions

As Akhenaten's new religion took hold, many local priests lost their positions or were coerced into **worshipping the Aten**. The king's administration demanded that all official inscriptions remove the plural form "gods," replacing it with the singular "god" (the Aten). Cartouches of Amun or other deities were **chiseled out**, and entire hieroglyphic phrases referencing them were destroyed.

This cultural purge affected everyday life: families who kept private shrines to household gods risked punishment if discovered. Soldiers posted in towns monitored compliance. People worried about neighbors snitching on them for maintaining small images of Ptah or Hathor. Some hid amulets or small statues, praying in secret. Fear of being labeled a heretic to the Aten overshadowed day-to-day routines. At the same time, plague or poor harvest could be misread as a sign that the old gods were punishing Egypt for abandoning them, fueling an atmosphere of **collective dread**.

12.6 The Impact on Death Rituals: A Terrifying Void

One of the most frightening changes was the confusion over **funeral practices**. Egyptians had long believed in elaborate ceremonies tied to gods like Osiris. Now, with Akhenaten dismissing these deities, families were unsure how to ensure a safe passage for the deceased. Did Osiris's role simply vanish? Was the Aten now responsible for judging souls?

The official line might have claimed that the Aten cared for everyone in the afterlife, but tradition-bound Egyptians found no comfort in this. Mummification workshops faced uncertainty—were the old prayers still valid? If not, were new prayers even created? The fear that a loved one's soul might be lost in the underworld, with no recognized god to guide it, terrified many. This spiritual turmoil further eroded public faith in Akhenaten's reforms.

12.7 Rumors of Disasters and Omens

During Akhenaten's reign, evidence suggests that a **plague** or epidemic struck parts of Egypt, possibly spreading from the Near East. Though details are sparse, the disease could have decimated the populace. Imagine the panic of an average villager: the old gods were banished, and now a deadly illness swept through. People might interpret this as proof that Amun and the others were **angry**, unleashing suffering because the pharaoh wrongfully suppressed their worship.

Signs of a failing economy—shortages of goods, inflation of prices—also appeared. Foreign relations became strained, as Akhenaten seemed less interested in defending Egypt's borders. Letters from vassal rulers, found in the **Amarna Tablets**, reveal pleas for military support against invasions. Some unanswered. Rumors of rebellious princes and lost territories circulated among Egyptian garrisons, who feared betrayal by a king more focused on religious experiments than on protecting the realm. This combination of **plague, economic trouble, and military neglect** added to the sense of gloom.

12.8 Life in Amarna: Forced Sunshine and Hidden Nightmares

Akhenaten's new capital, **Akhetaten**, was built to celebrate the sun's rays. Walls and stelae praised the Aten's daily rising and setting. But the reality for many inhabitants was far from idyllic. The land was hot, with little natural shade except the occasional garden. Laborers toiled in quarries to supply stone for temples, under a blazing sun that seemed merciless.

At night, the city might feel like a **ghost town**, with large open plazas and few traditional gods to comfort the devout. Soldiers patrolled the streets, ensuring that no secret shrines were erected under cover of darkness. Some citizens claimed to see **strange lights** in the sky—perhaps illusions caused by desert heat or flickers from distant watchfires. Others spoke of **unquiet spirits**, ghosts of those who had died unsettled in this new religious system. Whether based on reality or fear, these stories circulated widely, heightening the aura of oppression in Amarna.

12.9 Nefertiti's Role: Beauty and Fear

Queen **Nefertiti** played a prominent role in promoting the Aten. She appeared in reliefs conducting rituals alongside Akhenaten, wearing the same regalia as a priest. Some depictions even showed her smiting enemies, a traditionally royal (male) iconography. This shared power puzzled and alarmed those accustomed to seeing a clear division between the king's authority and a queen's supportive role.

To some, Nefertiti embodied **feminine grace** and was admired for her beauty, but her active involvement in suppressing old gods triggered whispers that she was a **sorceress** or a puppet of Akhenaten's radical cause. Others believed she possessed potent protective amulets from the Aten, making her nearly invincible. The line between admiration and fear was thin. The image of a strong queen siding with a single, newly proclaimed god felt unnatural to many, intensifying the anxiety that the natural order had been inverted.

12.10 Cracks in the Regime: Dissent in the Court

Not everyone at Amarna supported Akhenaten wholeheartedly. Some officials may have complied out of **fear**—fear of losing status, of incurring the king's wrath, or of being accused of treason against the Aten. A few tried to maintain double loyalty, quietly venerating the old gods while publicly praising the Aten. Royal storehouses, once stocked with wealth from Amun's temples, might be mismanaged, leading to corruption. In private letters, members of the administration expressed confusion or distress.

The army, in particular, felt neglected. Generals had trouble recruiting or supplying troops for border security. The chain of command might have been compromised by officers who resented the new religious orders. While open revolt did not break out (as far as records show), the tension simmered. The knowledge that so many disagreed with the king but remained silent built a climate of **paranoia**, as no one knew who might be a genuine supporter or who might be harboring rebellious thoughts.

12.11 Mysterious Disappearances and the Fear of Punishment

When a regime forcibly reshapes society, stories often arise of individuals who **vanish** under suspicious circumstances. Some might have been priests of the old gods who refused to adapt. Others could be local officials caught sabotaging the Aten's temples. Perhaps some high-ranking courtiers fell from favor for unknown reasons.

No official records detail mass purges, but the silence itself can be telling. Ancient scribes often covered up the darkest measures of a king. Rumors likely spread that certain temple guardians or devout Amun priests were exiled, jailed, or executed. The fear that one could be taken at night by royal guards made many keep their heads down, fueling the sense that the king or his close circle were capable of quiet, lethal retribution against dissenters.

12.12 Akhenaten's Apparent Indifference to Foreign Threats

Beyond the changes at home, letters from allied city-states in Canaan (the **Amarna Letters**) reveal urgent pleas for help against encroaching enemies like the Hittites. Some allied rulers wrote multiple times, complaining that Egyptian garrisons had not arrived, or that Akhenaten's officials refused to send supplies. Meanwhile, **vassal kings** turned traitor under outside pressure. This lack of strong foreign policy frightened Egyptian border troops, who risked being outnumbered or overtaken.

If news of defeats or lost territories reached the Egyptian heartland, commoners might interpret these setbacks as the result of deserting the old gods. Indeed, they might whisper that Amun had abandoned Egypt to foreign invaders. Soldiers who once felt pride in their powerful homeland saw it slipping away due to the king's religious obsession. This sense of betrayal and fear of defeat fanned the flames of anti-Akhenaten sentiment.

12.13 Late Reign: Illness, Isolation, and Eerie Omens

As Akhenaten's reign progressed (he ruled roughly from 1353 to 1336 BCE), the city of Amarna started to show **signs of fatigue**. Some buildings were left unfinished; others needed repairs but found no funding. The glamor of the early capital construction gave way to the **harsh reality** of sustaining life in an arid region with limited farmland.

Historical records hint that Akhenaten and some family members, possibly including daughters, fell ill. A plague or epidemic in the region could have heightened anxiety. The sudden or premature deaths in the royal family caused speculation that the old gods were **striking back**. Tomb scenes in Amarna show mourning for a princess. Meanwhile, Nefertiti's role becomes unclear—some theories suggest she vanished from records or took on a new name, possibly co-ruling with Akhenaten for a time. For the general populace, these royal tragedies were ominous signs, fueling the dread that the Aten's favor was waning or that the pantheon was punishing the heretical pharaoh.

12.14 Akhenaten's Death and the Collapse of the Aten Worship

Akhenaten died under uncertain circumstances, leaving the throne to a short-lived successor, **Smenkhkare**, and then to the boy-king **Tutankhaten** (soon renamed **Tutankhamun**). With Akhenaten gone, the entire system he had built around the Aten quickly unraveled. Priests, officials, and commoners rejoiced that they could **reopen** the temples of the old gods. The new king changed his name to Tutankhamun, symbolically restoring **Amun** to prominence.

In the aftermath, Egyptians eagerly **damned Akhenaten's memory**. They chiseled away his cartouches, destroyed his statues, and dismantled the city of Amarna. Once again, we see the concept of **damnatio memoriae**, the ultimate punishment: erasing someone's name to deny them a place in the afterlife. People who had feared retribution for years seized the chance to eradicate any sign of Akhenaten's heresy, hoping that by eliminating all traces, they would appease the gods. This violent backlash underscores how deeply his reforms had **terrified** the population and how powerful the cult of Amun still was.

12.15 Legacy: A Warning of Religious Extremes

In the grand scope of Egyptian history, Akhenaten's revolution was brief—lasting little more than 15 or so years. Yet its impact was profound. For a moment, Egypt witnessed what it meant for a single ruler to forcibly reshape religious life, discarding tradition in favor of a new, exclusive cult. The resulting fear spread through every corner of society: from priests robbed of their centuries-old roles, to peasants unsure how to bury their dead, to soldiers left exposed to foreign threats.

Later generations learned from this episode. Future pharaohs rarely attempted such sweeping religious changes again. The name "Akhenaten" was systematically stricken from official lists of kings. Even the location of Amarna became a ghost town. For centuries, Egyptians pretended he never existed. This **active erasure**—born from the terror he invoked—served as a cautionary tale about what happens when a king disrupts the delicate balance of the gods.

12.16 Religious Fear Beyond Akhenaten's Death

Although the old gods were restored, the **anxiety** that Akhenaten's heresy could have enduring consequences lingered. Some believed that his offense against Amun and the other gods would take generations to mend. Natural disasters, invasions, or plagues in subsequent eras might be attributed to the "taint" left behind by the heretic king. Superstition in Egyptian culture was strong—once trust in the cosmic order was broken, it was hard to fully repair.

Moreover, the reinstated priests of Amun likely used Akhenaten's downfall as a **warning**: it proved that any challenge to their god's primacy risked cosmic punishment. This argument would bolster Amun's priesthood in the late 18th Dynasty and beyond, allowing them to claim moral and religious high ground. The fear of repeating Akhenaten's mistake served as a powerful deterrent to any future pharaoh who might consider radical religious shifts.

12.17 Tomb Robberies and Ghost Stories in Amarna's Ruins

With the abandonment of Amarna, the tombs and buildings there became ripe for **robbery**. Tomb robbers likely looted any leftover goods, and over time, the city's empty streets developed a haunted reputation. Locals might venture there to scavenge stones or materials but speak of **ghostly apparitions** or curses left by Akhenaten's scribes. Some believed the restless spirits of those who died from plague wandered the desert plain, moaning for the old gods to forgive them.

These rumors added another layer of fear around Akhenaten's memory. Some travelers avoided the area altogether, not wanting to risk encountering these unquiet spirits or the wrath of any lingering Aten followers. This avoided region served as a testament to how one pharaoh's ambition to replace all gods with one could transform a prosperous capital into a spectral wasteland.

12.18 Tutankhamun's Restoration and the Slow Healing

The young king **Tutankhamun** (initially Tutankhaten) began a process of **restoration**—albeit overseen by powerful advisors like Ay and Horemheb. Temples to Amun were reopened, oracles resumed, and the people were encouraged to resume worship of multiple gods. Edicts were issued to reaffirm the old religion, hoping to **erase the fear** that had permeated society. Officials carefully dismantled the Aten temples, reusing the stones in other building projects.

Yet, healing took time. Generations had grown up under the Aten's monotheism. Soldiers who lost battles due to lack of support carried bitterness. Priests who had been persecuted found it hard to trust the monarchy. The fear that Egypt might again see such turmoil influenced political alliances and personal faith. People clung to Amun and the old gods even more fervently, perhaps in an effort to prove loyalty and avert any future disasters.

12.19 Aftermath and Reflection

Looking back, Egyptian historians of subsequent dynasties portrayed Akhenaten as a **monster** or, at best, a misguided fanatic. Some record him as a traitor to Maat—the sacred order of the cosmos. The extent of the erasure was so thorough that only fragmentary evidence remained, leading modern historians to piece together this chapter of Egyptian history centuries later.

For the ancient Egyptians who lived through it, Akhenaten's revolution was a time of **spiritual dread**. They had never faced such an abrupt, total reversal of their gods. The monarchy's power to shape religious practice revealed itself as a double-edged sword: while it could unify the land, it could also create intense fear and chaos if wielded to upend cherished beliefs. This cautionary note resonates throughout the rest of the New Kingdom and into the Late Period, showing how deeply an entire civilization could be shaken by one ruler's spiritual fervor.

CHAPTER 13

Tutankhamun's Tomb: Hidden Dangers and Ghostly Legends

Tutankhamun (c. 1336–1327 BCE) was a boy-king who ascended the throne during the tumultuous end of the 18th Dynasty. He was only around eight or nine years old when he became pharaoh, inheriting a kingdom that still reeled from Akhenaten's religious upheaval. When he died in his late teens, his successors hastily buried him in a modest tomb in the Valley of the Kings. Although much smaller than other royal tombs, it would become infamous many centuries later for its almost-intact treasures. Ancient Egyptians, too, whispered about what might lie within, telling ghostly tales and rumors of curses. This chapter explores how Tutankhamun's short reign sowed seeds of mystery, how his burial site was fraught with hidden dangers, and why stories of ghosts and curses emerged around his tomb, even in ancient times.

13.1 The Boy-King in a Land of Unrest

Tutankhamun was originally named **Tutankhaten**—a reflection of his father Akhenaten's devotion to the Aten. But soon after he took power, he changed his name to **Tutankhamun**, signaling a restoration of Amun's worship. Advisors like the influential priests and court officials—Ay, Horemheb, and others—likely guided him to do this, hoping to mend the breach between Amun's powerful cult and the throne. While these actions calmed some fears, the scars of Akhenaten's heresy still lingered. People worried about curses or divine punishment for those who had renounced the old gods.

Tutankhamun's youth added another layer of uncertainty. A child pharaoh might not command the same respect as a seasoned warrior-king. Rivals at court could conspire, or foreign enemies might test the kingdom's defenses. Though records are sparse, it's likely that the high priests and military officials formed a protective ring around Tutankhamun, controlling who could see him. This secrecy fueled rumors. Some citizens claimed the boy-king might be physically frail or under a "shadow" from the Aten fiasco. Others suggested that he carried the "sins" of his father's heresy and that ghosts of spurned gods haunted him.

These whispers never found official confirmation, but they underscored the superstitious climate surrounding his reign.

13.2 Sudden Death and a Hasty Burial

Tutankhamun died unexpectedly, around age eighteen or nineteen. The cause remains uncertain—some suspect an infection from a leg fracture, others suggest inherited illnesses or complications possibly linked to inbreeding. In any case, his passing caught the court off guard. A pharaoh's funeral usually took years of preparation, with elaborate tombs, statues, and funerary objects. But Tutankhamun's tomb, known today as **KV62** in the Valley of the Kings, appears relatively modest, suggesting a scramble to bury him properly with the limited time and materials available.

The need to bury a divine king swiftly was paramount in Egyptian tradition; delaying could invite a restless spirit or misfortune upon the living. So, priests, embalmers, and artisans worked day and night, placing gilded coffins, amulets, and provisions for the afterlife into a tomb never meant for a pharaoh. The corridors were cramped, and the painting was hasty. Officials might have worried that the unsettled spirit of Tutankhamun—unprepared for death—would wander if not given the essential funerary rites. Indeed, local rumors circulated that the boy-king's ghost might roam the desert, searching for the father he never properly buried (Akhenaten) or the gods he had to appease.

13.3 The Tomb's Layout: A Claustrophobic Labyrinth

Unlike grander tombs with multiple corridors and false chambers, Tutankhamun's tomb was small, consisting of a short descending corridor, an antechamber, a burial chamber, a treasury, and a side room (often called the annex). Because space was limited, items were crowded together—chariots, furniture, jars, statues—stacked haphazardly. For ancient Egyptians who guarded or entered the tomb soon after its sealing, the cramped darkness likely felt oppressive. Torchlight flickered on gilded shrines and the eerie painted walls.

The walls themselves depicted Tutankhamun's funeral procession and scenes of him with deities. But the corners might have loomed with shadows, and the stale air carried the scent of embalming resins. This claustrophobic environment led to stories that if someone entered uninvited, the tomb's narrow halls could **close in** on them, as if the walls themselves were alive with the spirit of the dead king. Superstitious guards believed that those who lingered too long risked hearing phantom footsteps behind them or glimpsing the faint outline of a boyish figure in the gloom.

13.4 Grave Robbers and the Early Curses

Tomb robbery was not a modern phenomenon. Even in Tutankhamun's time, thieves were a real threat. Papyrus documents from the late 18th and 19th Dynasties mention official investigations into tomb break-ins. While it seems that Tutankhamun's tomb was robbed briefly (perhaps twice in antiquity) soon after his burial—evidenced by disturbed items—those robbers likely stole small valuables and left before clearing the tomb completely. Why didn't they take it all?

Some speculate that a patrol or official guard may have chased them off. Others suspect the thieves were **frightened away**—either by real guards or by superstitious dread. Ancient Egyptians fully believed that a tomb's occupant could unleash curses upon any intruder. Statues of protective deities placed in the tomb, along with inscriptions, served as warnings. One formula might say: "Death shall come on swift wings to him who disturbs the peace of the king." Even if such texts were not precisely written in Tutankhamun's tomb (the actual curses are rarely direct), the cultural fear was enough. Thieves might have found the shimmering gold too enticing to resist initially—but upon hearing a strange echo or feeling an unexplained chill, they fled, convinced the spirit of the boy-king or an angry god was watching.

13.5 Protective Deities and Eerie Artwork

Scattered throughout the tomb were figures of gods and goddesses carved in wood, stone, or gold overlay, meant to guard Tutankhamun. Some displayed fierce animal heads—jackals, falcons, lions—signifying their power to ward off evildoers. In the treasury stood the iconic **golden shrine** containing the canopic chest, guarded by four goddesses (Isis, Nephthys, Selket, and Neith). Their outstretched arms seemed to embrace and protect the organs of the king, but to a fearful intruder, those arms looked like they might snare any trespasser.

The artwork on boxes and shrines displayed mythic battles: the king smiting foreign enemies or fighting chaotic animals representing evil forces. Ancient Egyptians interpreted these scenes as both real and symbolic—if Tutankhamun was shown defeating serpents or monstrous beings in the afterlife, it meant he could defeat tomb robbers, too. Legends told of serpents materializing inside the tomb to strike at thieves, or the painted enemies on the walls rising up to chase intruders through the darkness. Though rational minds might dismiss such tales, the power of suggestion in a dark, enclosed space was strong.

13.6 Ghostly Legends and The Young Pharaoh's Restless Spirit

Because Tutankhamun died so young, stories arose that he might have had **unfinished business**. Some believed he was cheated out of a full reign, which might leave his spirit longing for the sunlight he rarely knew as a sickly child. Rumors said that on certain nights, near the Valley of the Kings, a faint, boyish figure could be seen wandering the cliffs, carrying a torch or searching for lost companions. Local workers or guards, who spent nights in huts near the tombs, sometimes claimed to hear distant crying or moaning carried on the wind.

Over time, these ghostly tales merged with the broader tradition of **ka** (spiritual double) hauntings. Egyptians believed the ka could roam if the funerary rites were insufficient or if the tomb was desecrated. If a guard or worker fell ill after patrolling near Tutankhamun's tomb, superstitious peers might blame the boy-king's restless spirit. A small cut that turned infected could be taken as proof of the tomb's curse. Though we lack direct textual evidence of these exact legends, the cultural context strongly supports that rumors of **phantoms** and **vengeful spirits** swirled around any royal burial considered "unfinished" or "unusual."

13.7 The High Priests and the Suppression of Rumors

Priests from the Temple of Amun, seeking to uphold the monarchy's image, likely tried to quell such ghost stories. They had a vested interest in maintaining reverence for the pharaoh, even a deceased boy-king. Official proclamations might have stated that Tutankhamun was at peace with the gods, that his tomb was sealed by divine command, and that no harm would come to those who respected the burial site. Yet, these proclamations were overshadowed by the deep-seated Egyptian belief in **curses** and **vengeful afterlife powers**.

If a local farmer claimed to see a ghostly child near the tomb's entrance at night, temple scribes could punish him for spreading falsehoods or accuse him of tomb-robbing intentions. Fear of official retribution and fear of the tomb's curse thus created a dual layer of dread—people stayed away, neither wanting to face the king's wrath from beyond nor the priests' wrath in the earthly realm. This uneasy stalemate helped preserve Tutankhamun's tomb from large-scale looting for a while, though minor thefts still occurred in the more chaotic periods that followed.

13.8 Posthumous Reputation: A Minor King with a Major Curse

As centuries passed, Tutankhamun faded into near-obscurity, overshadowed by more famous rulers like Thutmose III, Seti I, and Ramses II. But in local folklore, the boy-king's tomb sometimes featured in cautionary tales: the story of a reckless man who tried to break in and lost his mind; or the legend of a petty thief who stole a small statue, only to be found dead under mysterious circumstances the next day. These tales might have been recycled from general tomb-curse narratives, but attaching them to a youthful, tragic ruler made them all the more poignant.

Interestingly, when later pharaohs in the 19th and 20th Dynasties refurbished tombs or moved mummies to safer caches, they seemed to leave Tutankhamun's resting place relatively undisturbed. Perhaps they deemed it unremarkable, or maybe they, too, feared tampering with a tomb rumored to be guarded by an especially restless spirit. Although we lack direct evidence of "Tutankhamun curses" from the period, the general Egyptian mindset strongly suggests that his tomb was considered **dangerous** to meddle with.

13.9 Medical Mysteries and Mummy Maladies

Ancient Egyptians believed that mummies radiated a kind of supernatural power. Embalming materials like natron, resins, and oils had symbolic potency. A royal mummy could be even more potent because it was a vessel for a king's ba (soul) and ka. If the mummy was disturbed—unwrapped or touched without proper rituals—catastrophe might follow. Some Egyptians believed that diseases could jump from the decaying flesh to the living, like a spiritual contamination. This was a **real fear** that combined basic knowledge of infection with religious dread of cursed remains.

For a young, possibly frail pharaoh like Tutankhamun, rumors might have circulated that his own illnesses or hereditary issues lingered in his mummy, ready to afflict anyone who dared to disturb the coffin. The presence of precious amulets meant to protect him in the afterlife further heightened the idea that powerful charms and incantations were at play. Removing or damaging them could release dark forces. In times of plague or strange outbreaks, people near the Valley of the Kings might recall such beliefs, blaming misfortunes on tomb disturbance—real or rumored.

13.10 Later Efforts to Secure the Tomb

Various Egyptian rulers tried to reorganize the Valley of the Kings' security, especially during the 19th and 20th Dynasties when tomb robberies became rampant. The idea was to post guards, erect hidden entrances, or create official necropolis police forces. While Tutankhamun's tomb was not the grandest, it still contained gold funerary objects that unscrupulous officials or bandits coveted. Thus, from time to time, the necropolis administration might have sealed off side passages leading toward KV62, set curses or warnings at the entrances, or rearranged corridors to confuse any intruder.

One can imagine a foreman telling his workers: "The boy-king's tomb is under special watch tonight. No one goes near. The gods themselves stand guard." This blend of official guard duty and religious intimidation served to dissuade theft. Meanwhile, the local population might have whispered that the tomb needed no guard, for the child-pharaoh's ghost roamed within, punishing trespassers more surely than any living watchman.

13.11 The Evolving Myth of Tutankhamun

Over time, as the New Kingdom declined and gave way to foreign invasions in later eras, many details about Tutankhamun were lost. But the kernel of a **mythic narrative** lingered: a boy-king who died too soon, was buried in haste, and guarded by formidable curses. This made for a potent story in a culture that already placed high value on funeral rites and the afterlife.

In an era when daily life was fraught with uncertainties—famine, war, disease—Egyptians found cautionary tales useful. They served as moral lessons, warning: "Do not stray from the path of piety, or the vengeful spirits of kings may find you." For that reason, Tutankhamun's tomb was left mostly sealed and hidden, passing through history with a shadowy reputation. Even though it did not stand out among the grand monuments of Thebes, it held a special aura of **the unknown**—the perfect breeding ground for ghostly legends.

CHAPTER 14

The Rameses Era: Clash of Empires and Horrors of War

The aftermath of Tutankhamun's death saw power shift to strong rulers like Ay and Horemheb, who attempted to stabilize Egypt by reinstating traditional religion and recovering from the chaos of the late 18th Dynasty. Then came the 19th Dynasty, founded by **Rameses I**, followed quickly by **Seti I** and, most famously, **Rameses II** (Ramses the Great). This era, often collectively referred to as the "Rameses era," featured extensive military campaigns, monumental building projects, and a sense that Egypt was once again a formidable empire. However, behind the grand temples and colossal statues lay terrifying realities: forced labor, massive casualties in war, and the looming threat of foreign powers. In this chapter, we will explore the **darker side** of the Rameses period, revealing the horrors of warfare, violent conquests, and the use of fear to maintain an empire's hold over its territories.

14.1 Rise of a New Dynasty: Securing Power through Force

Rameses I served briefly, establishing a new line, but his successor, **Seti I** (c. 1290–1279 BCE), truly began the transformation. Seti I's reign focused on restoring Egypt's borders, reasserting dominance over territories lost or neglected during Akhenaten's time. Campaigns into Syria-Palestine and Libya brought swift, brutal actions. Documents record Seti I leading armies that clashed with local chieftains, punishing dissent and extracting tribute.

The Egyptian army at this stage was a well-organized force, equipped with **chariots**, composite bows, spears, and axes. Skilled in formations and quick strikes, they could terrorize smaller city-states. After capturing a town, the Egyptians might parade local leaders as hostages, or in worse cases, put them to the sword. Civilians were subjected to mass deportations or forced labor if they resisted. Indeed, the success of these campaigns rested not just on Egypt's skill in battle but on the **fear** they instilled: if a city revolted, it faced the fate of total destruction, and its population risked enslavement.

14.2 Rameses II: The Self-Proclaimed Invincible

Rameses II (c. 1279–1213 BCE) carried Seti I's imperial ambitions to new heights. He constructed colossal monuments—like the Ramesseum in Thebes and the rock-cut temples at Abu Simbel—displaying enormous statues of himself. These projects aimed to awe both Egyptians and foreign visitors. But behind the grandeur, conscripted laborers toiled under harsh conditions. Many were peasants forced from their fields, risking hunger at home. Others might have been prisoners of war, working in quarries or hauling massive stones in scorching heat. Overseers punished disobedience or slowness with whippings and withheld rations, fostering an atmosphere of **terror** at the building sites.

Meanwhile, Rameses II's most famous military engagement was the **Battle of Kadesh** against the Hittites (c. 1274 BCE). Egyptian records, especially on temple walls, depict a heroic Rameses singlehandedly winning the day. But in reality, the battle seems to have been a **brutal stalemate** with high casualties. Soldiers found themselves caught in ambushes, chariots clashing in dusty chaos, and entire units wiped out. Survivors carried memories of severed limbs, trampled bodies, and the shrieks of horses and men. While Rameses boasted of victory, the cost in Egyptian lives was enormous. Fear of the Hittite war machine grew, especially among border garrisons who realized the empire's might was not always unstoppable.

14.3 Horrors on the Battlefield: Chariots and Casualties

Chariot warfare exemplified the **fierceness** of the Late Bronze Age. Egyptian chariots typically carried two men: a driver and an archer or spearman. They galloped across the battlefield, unleashing arrows or spears before darting away. Enemies who lacked chariots faced a terrifying sight—swift-moving platforms of death bearing down on them. The dust and thunder of hooves could shatter morale. Soldiers pinned on the ground might be run over, dying under chariot wheels or impaled by spears.

When an Egyptian army overcame a foe, they sometimes displayed war trophies—**severed hands** or phalli from fallen enemies—to count the dead and prove their success to the king. Wall reliefs in temples show pharaohs receiving piles of these grisly tokens. Such images served as propaganda but also as a stark reminder that defiance brought annihilation. The psychological impact of these displays on both Egyptians and their enemies was profound: to fight Egypt was to risk total destruction, bodily mutilation, and eternal dishonor.

14.4 The Fate of Prisoners and Foreign Captives

Conquest led to the capture of thousands of prisoners—men, women, and children—who became the pharaoh's property. Some were assigned to temple estates as laborers, forced to work fields or tend animals. Others were dispatched to quarries and mines, where the grueling labor and dangerous conditions meant a short life expectancy. Egyptian inscriptions might boast about bringing "countless captives" from foreign lands, parading them before the pharaoh.

Behind these triumphal claims lay **human misery**: families torn apart, children sold as household servants, survivors branded or tattooed to mark them as property. The threat of harsh punishments—beatings, starvation, or summary executions—ensured submission. Over time, some captives assimilated into Egyptian society, but many remained second-class residents, living in fear of being punished for any perceived disloyalty. The empire thus expanded not just through treaties but by populating its labor force with traumatized prisoners of war who served as living proof of pharaoh's might.

14.5 Defensive Fortresses: Walls that Kept People In

Rameses II and his successors built or renovated **fortresses** across the empire's frontiers—especially in Nubia to the south, along the Sinai routes, and near the eastern Delta facing Asia. While these structures were meant to keep hostile forces out, they also policed and restricted local populations. Garrison commanders wielded authority over trade caravans, controlling who could pass and demanding tolls or bribes. Local inhabitants learned to fear the fortress guards, who had the power to seize goods or conscript workers at will.

Egypt's fortress system supported a culture of **vigilance and suspicion**. Spies or scouts reported any sign of rebellion, and the response could be immediate and brutal. The local people in border regions lived under a double threat: foreign raiders on one side, and Egyptian fort garrisons on the other. At times, entire villages might be relocated if the authorities deemed them security risks. This policy created resentment, fueling small-scale revolts that were in turn crushed, perpetuating the cycle of **fear and suppression**.

14.6 The Cult of Personality: Rameses II as a Living God

Like many pharaohs, Rameses II was associated with divine lineage. But his self-promotion went beyond the norm. Temples across Egypt displayed colossal statues of Rameses merged with deities like Ra or Amun. In official hymns, scribes praised him as the "strong bull," "beloved of Maat," and sometimes gave him credit for the rising sun and the flood of the Nile. Commoners were encouraged to see him as a **semi-divine** figure whose very presence ensured prosperity.

Yet, behind the facade of divine kingship lurked a **tyrannical potential**: if you angered a living god, the consequences could be catastrophic. Local governors knew that failing to send enough tribute or manpower could result in severe punishment. Temple priests found themselves in precarious positions—while they revered Amun, they also had to integrate worship of Rameses's divine aspect. Dissenting voices might be branded as heretics or traitors, disappearing quietly from public life.

14.7 Forced Labor for Monumental Projects

Rameses II embarked on massive building campaigns, from adding new pylons at Karnak Temple to erecting the **colossal statues at Abu Simbel**. For these constructions, an immense labor force was needed. While some workers might have been paid laborers or skilled artisans, a significant portion were likely **conscripted peasants** or prisoners of war.

Teams dragged enormous stone blocks across the desert heat. Injuries were common—dislocated limbs, crushed bones from accidents, dehydration, and infections. Overseers maintained order with whips or rods, threatening to reduce rations if quotas were not met. The daily terror for a worker was tangible: fail to haul your assigned block, or show signs of exhaustion, and you faced punishment that could range from beatings to permanent disability. Meanwhile, the grandeur of the monuments stood as a testament to the pharaoh's glory and as a stark symbol of the **fear-based** labor system that built them.

14.8 Diplomacy by Intimidation: Treaties and Threats

While Rameses II eventually concluded a **peace treaty** with the Hittites—often cited as one of the earliest surviving written treaties—getting to that point involved intimidation, posturing, and further warfare. Egyptian scribes glorified Rameses's battlefield prowess, sending a message to other powers: defy Egypt at your peril. Envoys from smaller states in Canaan, for instance, were acutely aware of what had happened to rebellious cities in the past, where houses were burned, and survivors enslaved.

This style of diplomacy by intimidation meant local rulers sometimes acted loyal to Egypt out of sheer terror. They paid tribute, offered hostages, and paraded Egyptian symbols to avoid retribution. Of course, resentment simmered beneath the surface. Occasional uprisings or conspiracies arose, prompting fresh military interventions. The cycle of fear continued, with conquered peoples always cautious about stepping out of line, and Egyptian forces always ready to strike with merciless force if they did.

14.9 Internal Propaganda and the Shadow of War

Inside Egypt, the monarchy promoted narratives of **unbeatable armies** and a heroic king. Temples featured reliefs of Rameses II driving enemies before him. Priests choreographed festivals celebrating "divine victories," while scribes recorded flattering accounts of battles. Yet, soldiers returning from war might bear wounds or speak in hushed tones about the horrors they witnessed: villages set aflame, piles of corpses, the screams of the dying. The monarchy suppressed such stories to keep morale high.

For ordinary Egyptians, the knowledge that their pharaoh was waging constant campaigns could breed anxiety: if the empire stretched itself too thin, might foreigners invade the homeland? Or if tribute demands grew heavier to fund campaigns, might peasants starve or lose their land? Meanwhile, veterans who had seen war's brutality could struggle to integrate back into civilian life, haunted by nightmares. The state had no concept of mental health support—these men either conformed or risked punishment for dissent. Fear was a unifying force, ironically binding the populace to the pharaoh's strategy while also fostering a silent dread that any new war could be their last.

14.10 The Use of Magic and Superstition in Warfare

Egyptian generals, including those under Rameses II, commonly employed **religious and magical rites** before battle. They sacrificed animals to ensure the favor of the gods, recited incantations to protect soldiers from enemy arrows, and painted amulets with spells to ward off harm. Some believed that these spells could incapacitate the enemy or ensure Egyptian arrows flew true.

On the battlefield, these beliefs added a psychological edge. If Egyptian troops believed they were shielded by divine magic, they might fight with greater ferocity. Conversely, their adversaries might be intimidated, certain that the Egyptians had the backing of potent gods. Yet, when battles turned bloody or indecisive, superstitious soldiers could experience deep despair—wondering if some hidden curse or foreign deity's wrath had broken the protective spells. Anxiety about hidden magic from the opposing side also played a role, with claims that Hittite sorcerers could conjure illusions or storms to disrupt Egyptian chariots. War, in this sense, became a **clash of invisible forces** as much as a collision of spears and arrows.

14.11 Civilian Impact: Raids and Reprisals

Large-scale warfare inevitably spilled over into civilian areas. Campaigns by Rameses II or his successors might involve crossing enemy territory, where Egyptian soldiers would requisition food, animals, and sometimes people. If locals resisted, houses were torched and fields devastated, leaving survivors to starve. For peasants, hearing that an Egyptian army approached could be as frightening as hearing that a foreign army was near—both sides could be brutal if they suspected collaboration with the enemy.

Even within Egypt, people along the desert edges or near the Delta border lived in constant readiness, unsure if the next conflict might roll across their farms. Some tried to flee deeper into the Nile Valley, causing waves of refugees. Others formed militia groups or cooperated with the Egyptian forces in hopes of leniency. The monarchy might label these migrations as disloyal or traitorous if they seemed unorganized. Fear governed civilians' choices, as they weighed the lesser evil: stay and risk conflict at home, or move and risk punishment as deserters.

14.12 Aftermath of Conquests: Gloating Temples and Unheard Cries

When a pharaoh returned victorious, a grand ceremony took place. Priests hosted thanksgiving rituals; scribes composed triumphant hymns, and public celebrations were held. Temples displayed new reliefs showing the pharaoh's might, with rows of captives or piles of enemy arms. But the voices of the conquered rarely appeared in these records. No official stela recounted the burning of villages or the sorrow of enslaved mothers and children. Egyptian propaganda glorified the empire's expansion while silencing the anguish it caused.

Among the populace, these official celebrations reinforced the idea that war was both holy and inevitable. People cheered the pharaoh's might, half-knowing that somewhere far away, entire cities lay in ruins. Fear also kept them from questioning the morality of these campaigns. Any doubt expressed could be interpreted as disloyalty to the throne—punishable by confiscation of property, forced labor, or worse.

14.13 The Legacy of Rameses II's Military Might

Rameses II lived to an old age, his reign lasting about sixty-six years. During this time, Egypt maintained a vast empire, but the cost in human lives was tremendous. In many ways, Rameses's presence overshadowed the entire 19th Dynasty. After his death, successor pharaohs like **Merneptah** and others had to contend with new enemies and internal strife. The fear-based methods—mass deportations, forced labor, savage reprisals—remained standard practice.

Over time, as the 19th Dynasty waned and the 20th began, resources were stretched thin. Tomb robberies in the Valley of the Kings surged, internal power struggles increased, and foreign threats multiplied. The seeds of Egypt's eventual decline were sown in part by the constant militarization and reliance on terror tactics. Soldiers and statesmen who knew only conquest could not easily transition to an era of peace and economic reform. Fear was so ingrained that it shaped foreign and domestic policies for generations to come.

14.14 Seti II, Siptah, and the Growing Chaos

Following Rameses II's long reign, his descendants grappled for control. **Seti II** (c. 1200–1194 BCE) faced rebellions and court intrigues. **Siptah** was a young king with a crippled foot, possibly a result of polio, who died before stabilizing the realm. During these successions, the empire's grip on distant territories loosened, encouraging local revolts. Egyptian forces still tried to crush uprisings, but the treasury was no longer as flush with spoils of war, and corruption in the necropolis and administrative offices soared.

Internal documents mention stolen goods from royal tombs and bribes paid to officials who turned a blind eye. Even priests in high positions exploited their temple wealth for personal gain. This climate of moral decay reflected the inherent **instability** of a state built on intimidation. When a strong pharaoh like Rameses II was absent, fear alone could not hold everything together. The petty horrors of local power-hungry officials inflicted daily miseries: forced labor quotas soared, taxation became ever more brutal, and entire communities lived on the edge of despair.

14.15 Religious Tensions and Growing Desperation

As the monarchy struggled, the **Cult of Amun** and other powerful priesthoods sometimes clashed with the royal court. Each side tried to claim the gods' favor, occasionally using oracles to condemn political rivals. People feared the return of a crisis like the Amarna period, though no pharaoh tried to reinstate monotheism. Instead, the fear was more about power grabs: if priests gained too much influence, they might overshadow the king again, or if the king tried to curb the priests, civil strife could erupt.

Meanwhile, the lower classes felt squeezed. In times of famine or poor Nile floods, they looked to local temples for relief. But temple granaries and storehouses often operated under heavy guard, distributing supplies only in carefully controlled ways. Some peasants accused temple officials of hoarding or theft. Rumors flared that the gods were punishing Egypt for its wars and cruelty. A sense of cosmic dread pervaded the land: maybe the endless cycle of conquest and oppression had broken the divine order (Maat), inviting chaos (Isfet) in response.

14.16 Tomb Building in the Late 19th and 20th Dynasties: Heightened Fear

Despite the empire's troubles, pharaohs continued to build elaborate tombs in the Valley of the Kings. With each new tomb, priests and architects introduced more elaborate **curses** and protective texts, perhaps reflecting the heightened paranoia of the age. Walls showed horrifying demons punishing the unworthy in the afterlife. Some spells specifically threatened tomb robbers, promising they would be devoured by serpents or tormented by soul-eating monsters.

These inscriptions were not just for the pharaoh's safe passage; they served as deterrents. Word spread among workers that the supernatural guardians in these tombs had grown fiercer. Some said they heard moans or roars echoing through newly carved chambers. The combination of real security measures (like hidden passages) and chilling magical warnings created an atmosphere where even official tomb-builders might avoid entering certain corridors alone. Fear was layered: fear of mortal punishment by the pharaoh's men, and fear of immortal punishment by underworld deities.

14.17 The Shifting Balance of Power: Merneptah and Ramesses III

Merneptah (c. 1213–1203 BCE), one of Rameses II's younger sons, faced invasions by the so-called "Sea Peoples" and internal revolts in Canaan. His victory inscriptions bragged of crushing enemies, but the reality was a battered Egypt struggling to fend off waves of outsiders. The empire's foundation of intimidation still functioned, yet cracks appeared. Each new foe tested Egypt's stamina.

Later, **Ramesses III** of the 20th Dynasty tried to emulate Rameses the Great, waging wars against the Sea Peoples and in Nubia. He boasted of success, but draining resources and rising corruption plagued his reign. At Medinet Habu, the mortuary temple of Ramesses III, extensive reliefs celebrate victories, including piles of enemy hands and heads. However, behind these grand images lay more forced labor, higher taxes, and severe social unrest. Eventually, Ramesses III fell victim to a **harem conspiracy**, in which one of his wives and palace officials plotted to kill him—proof that fear worked both ways, breeding treachery within the royal household itself.

14.18 Civilian Revolts and Strikes

Even under the iron fist of the Rameses kings, civilians sometimes revolted. One famous example is the **Deir el-Medina strike** (c. 1152 BCE) during Ramesses III's reign, where tomb artisans and workers walked off the job because they had not been paid their rations of grain. This was the first recorded strike in history. Workers overcame their fear of punishment because hunger and desperation outweighed everything else.

Armed guards tried to control the strikers, but the workers appealed to local administrators, even writing petitions on papyri. Eventually, the authorities had to appease them, delivering overdue food. This strike underscored how the constant pressure of war, taxes, and forced labor frayed the social fabric. Fear alone could not keep people from rebelling when their basic survival was threatened.

14.19 Gradual Decline and the End of an Era

By the late 20th Dynasty (c. 1070 BCE), the New Kingdom crumbled into the **Third Intermediate Period**. Egypt no longer dominated foreign lands as it once did. Internal divisions saw the rise of powerful High Priests of Amun in Thebes, essentially splitting the country. The Rameses line died out, replaced by weaker claimants. Tomb robberies reached epidemic levels as the central government lost control.

Historians look back at this era as a lesson in how an empire built on conquest and intimidation can unravel. While Rameses II's achievements were monumental, the system that upheld them bred deep-seated fear, oppression, and an overextended military apparatus. The horrors of war took their toll, and the forced labor economy contributed to social unrest. When strong leadership failed, the empire's structure could not stand on mere terror. Local rebellions, corruption, and external threats converged, signaling the end of the powerful New Kingdom state.

CHAPTER 15

The Late Period: Invasions, Destructions, and Dark Omens

By the end of the New Kingdom, Egypt's grip on its empire had weakened. Internal strife, economic troubles, and corruption eroded the power of the central government. Foreign armies and ambitious warlords recognized Egypt's vulnerability. Soon, new dynasties, many of them foreign-born, rose and fell with alarming speed. This era of **the Late Period** (about 747–332 BCE) was marked by repeated invasions—Nubians, Assyrians, and later Persians—each leaving a trail of destruction. Large stretches of the Nile Valley were ravaged. Sacred temples were looted; entire families were displaced. Egyptians lived under the shadow of continuous threat, reading every eclipse, every flood, and every plague as a possible omen of impending doom.

In this chapter, we explore the **scary side** of the Late Period: violent takeovers, savage reprisals, betrayals among high priests and governors, and a growing sense that the gods themselves might be abandoning the land. We will witness how fear settled deep into the hearts of Egyptian rulers and commoners alike. From once-mighty cities reduced to rubble, to priests who turned to dark oracles in desperate attempts to repel invaders, the Late Period stands as a stark reminder of how easily an ancient civilization can become haunted by its own vulnerability.

15.1 Egypt's Fractured Political Landscape

After the collapse of the New Kingdom, Egypt fell into divisions. Some local rulers claimed the title of pharaoh, but they had little power outside their home districts. Nomarchs (governors) behaved like petty kings. The priesthood of Amun in Thebes also claimed spiritual control. This chaotic patchwork of authorities left the land fragile and open to attack. Ordinary Egyptians felt constant anxiety. Who truly ruled the country? Would taxes go to the local lord or some distant king? And how could families protect themselves if war erupted overnight?

Amid this turmoil, brigands and mercenary bands roamed the desert edges, sometimes hired by local chiefs to settle disputes, other times living as marauders. The streets of once-orderly cities could become warzones if rival claimants clashed. Temples tried to maintain stability, but priests themselves were often entangled in power struggles, using **curses** or oracles to legitimize their chosen ruler. The sense of a unified, invincible Egypt was gone. Citizens glanced nervously at the horizon, expecting foreign powers to exploit this confusion.

15.2 The Nubian Conquest and a Hopeful Restoration

One of the earliest foreign powers to seize the moment was **Nubia** (Kush), south of Egypt. Nubians had longstanding cultural ties with Egypt but also a history of conflict. Around 747 BCE, the Nubian king **Piye** (or Piankhi) marched north, claiming he would restore true worship of Amun and end the decadent behavior of local Egyptian rulers. Many Egyptians, weary of the chaos, actually welcomed Piye as a possible savior. Nubian rule, at first, seemed like it might bring stability and a renewed devotion to the old gods.

Yet, not everyone embraced the Kushite Dynasty. Certain Delta rulers resisted Piye's forces fiercely, leading to battles near Memphis and other key cities. Accounts from Piye's own stela boast of enemies "choking on their own blood." Rumors circulated that Piye's priests placed curses on rebellious governors, condemning them to diseases or nightmares. Fear of Nubian retaliation drove many city officials to surrender without a fight. Still, once Piye left, Egyptian dynasts in the north tried to reassert autonomy. This back-and-forth created an uneasy atmosphere: at any moment, an armed force might appear, demanding loyalty—or heads would roll.

15.3 Religious Zeal or Tyranny? The Nubian Pharaohs' Grip

The Nubian pharaohs saw themselves as reformers, purging corruption from Amun's temples. In Thebes, high priests found new patrons in these southern kings. Yet, with religious zeal came harsh punishments for those deemed blasphemous or unholy. Some local cults, especially those honoring minor gods, felt persecuted. Nubian soldiers occasionally attacked shrines that they believed practiced questionable rituals. Accusations of **dark sorcery** were used to justify violent crackdowns.

Those who opposed Nubian rule risked being labeled enemies of Amun. This charge could result in torture or death. City dwellers whispered that resistance leaders vanished in the night. Some claimed to hear screams echoing from fortress dungeons. The line between pious renewal and tyrannical oppression was blurred. While many Egyptians appreciated the Nubian desire for religious purity, they could not ignore the sense of dread that accompanied it. Every new edict from the Nubian court might carry a hidden threat.

15.4 The Assyrian Invasion: A Storm from the East

As the Nubian kings tried to unify Egypt, a far more terrifying force loomed on the eastern horizon: the **Assyrian Empire**. The Assyrians were renowned (or infamous) for their ruthless war tactics—impaling prisoners, sacking cities, and deporting entire populations. Hearing rumors of Egypt's wealth and chaos, the Assyrians launched several campaigns. King **Esarhaddon** led one such invasion in the early 7th century BCE, crossing the Sinai and smashing through Delta strongholds.

Egyptian accounts, though scarce, describe panic sweeping the countryside. Citizens fled their homes, carrying what little they could. The Assyrians systematically sacked towns, destroyed temples, and captured local leaders. Even sacred statues of the gods were taken as trophies back to Assyria. For Egyptians, this was an unthinkable humiliation: images of their deities held hostage in foreign lands. Tales of **atrocities** spread quickly: entire families slain, survivors forced into slave caravans. Nubian-led armies tried to repel the Assyrians but found themselves outmatched by advanced iron weaponry and cruel tactics. The invaders left behind a scarred landscape littered with corpses and burned ruins—eerie reminders that no city, not even Memphis, was safe.

15.5 Destruction of Temples and the Loss of Ancient Wisdom

One of the most frightening consequences of these invasions was the **destruction of temples**—not just as centers of worship but as repositories of knowledge. Scribes stored scrolls, medical recipes, magical spells, and genealogies in temple libraries. Invaders saw them as symbols of Egyptian pride and burned them to break morale. When libraries went up in flames, centuries of accumulated wisdom about astronomy, medicine, ritual, and architecture vanished overnight.

Priests who survived often fled to remote regions, clutching fragments of sacred texts. Some tried to preserve knowledge by teaching it orally to a select few. But the damage was immense, fueling the sense that the gods themselves might be punishing Egypt. If the sacred words were lost, how could the dead find safe passage in the afterlife? How could priests perform essential rites to stave off chaos? Rumors circulated of entire cities left "spiritually naked," their protective spells undone, leaving them open to curses and plagues.

15.6 Assyrian Rule and the Seeds of Rebellion

For a time, **Assyrian vassal kings** ruled parts of Egypt, while Nubian forces held out in the south. This dual occupation deepened the feeling of hopelessness among ordinary Egyptians. Assyrian garrisons extracted heavy tribute—grain, gold, slaves. Local officials who cooperated with Assyrian governors were viewed with suspicion by their own people. Secret rebel groups formed, sharing coded messages on scraps of papyrus. Anyone caught conspiring might be tortured or impaled as a warning to others.

The environment buzzed with **paranoia**. Neighbors turned on neighbors, hoping to curry favor with the authorities or to deflect suspicion from themselves. Temples tried to keep religious services going, but attendance dropped. Many worshipers feared that showing too much piety to Amun or other gods could mark them as potential rebels. Meanwhile, seers interpreted every natural anomaly—like a solar eclipse or an unusually low Nile flood—as a sign that the cosmic balance was shattered, further stoking dread.

15.7 The Rise of Psamtik I and an Egyptian Revival

Eventually, cracks in the Assyrian Empire and strategic alliances allowed an ambitious local prince named **Psamtik I** (of the 26th Dynasty) to expel foreign garrisons. He united much of Egypt around 664 BCE, forging a Saite dynasty that aimed to restore Egypt's fortunes. At first, this seemed like a bright dawn. Psamtik rebuilt temples, revived trade in the Mediterranean, and hired Greek mercenaries to bolster his army. People dared to hope that Egypt could recover its old splendor.

Yet, behind this optimism lurked a **haunting memory** of repeated invasions. Fear shaped Psamtik's policies. He kept a tight grip on local governors, suspecting them of potential betrayal. Greek mercenaries patrolled city walls, their foreign speech adding an unsettling edge. Some Egyptians murmured that relying on foreign soldiers was an omen of future betrayals. Priests, too, walked a careful path: they welcomed Psamtik's patronage but worried another invasion might strike if the gods were offended again. A cloud of tension remained, as if the land itself held its breath, waiting for the next disaster.

15.8 Encounters with the Persians: A New Menace

The next major wave of fear arrived in the form of the **Persian Empire** under Cambyses II and later Darius I. By 525 BCE, Persian armies overwhelmed Egyptian defenses at Pelusium in the Delta. Legends say the Persians used cats and other sacred animals as shields, knowing Egyptians hesitated to harm creatures associated with their gods. Whether myth or fact, the story highlighted Egypt's vulnerability to psychological warfare. After Pelusium fell, the rest of the country followed swiftly.

Persian rule proved harsh. Cambyses reportedly looted temples, mocked Egyptian customs, and even killed the Apis bull (a sacred embodiment of Ptah) in Memphis. Though some historians debate the details, Egyptians widely believed Cambyses had committed sacrilege. They saw the land sinking deeper into **divine disfavor**. The dreaded stories of Persian cruelty—public floggings, forced marches to Asia, confiscation of temple lands—spread terror across the Nile Valley. Under Darius, conditions stabilized somewhat, but the fear that foreigners controlled the Two Lands rankled Egyptians, who longed for independence.

15.9 Rebellions and Bloody Crackdowns

Egyptians did not passively accept Persian domination. Multiple revolts flared, often led by native princes or ambitious generals claiming the gods' blessing. One such uprising in the Delta gained momentum before Persian forces retaliated, slaughtering rebels and taking hostages. Entire districts were burned, and local temples ransacked again. Survivors recounted grim scenes: piles of bodies in temple courtyards, rivers choked with dead fish feeding on corpses. In the aftermath, Persian officials tightened their grip, imposing heavier taxes to punish rebellious provinces.

These crackdowns amplified the sense of **hopeless terror**. Parents told children to remain silent about any anti-Persian sentiment. Secret cells of rebels still formed in distant oases, but few dared to join unless they were desperate. The knowledge of Persian retribution—impalements, flayings, and mass enslavement—was enough to keep most Egyptians subdued. Meanwhile, oracles that once guided rebellions now fell silent or gave ambiguous messages, perhaps fearing Persian spies or simply losing confidence that the gods supported another failed uprising.

15.10 The Libyan and Greek Interferences

Amid Persian dominance, other forces also meddled. Libyan tribes in the west raided border towns. Greek city-states, seeking influence or trade opportunities, sometimes supported local Egyptian warlords. This external interference further fragmented the land. Each foreign group demanded tribute or a share of the Nile's riches. Egyptians trapped in border regions found themselves paying multiple overlords—Persians on one side, Libyans on another, and Greek mercenaries roaming the trade routes.

Local stories described the plight of farmers robbed multiple times per season. If they refused, their fields were torched. If they collaborated with one side, they risked vengeance from another. People felt the gods had abandoned them. Some turned to lesser-known deities or **magical cults**, hoping for protection. Tales of new curses and hidden rituals emerged, as priests claimed they had discovered "forbidden spells" to curse invaders. Yet, these rumors rarely stopped the violence. Fear reigned supreme, overshadowing any illusions of a quick restoration of Egyptian autonomy.

15.11 Economic Decay and Social Unrest

Long-standing wars and occupations drained Egypt's coffers. Trade routes were disrupted or heavily taxed by foreign powers. Farms neglected during repeated conflicts led to smaller harvests. Many peasants fell into debt, sometimes selling themselves or their children into **bondage**. Scenes of beggars lining temple avenues, or entire villages abandoned, became more common. High priests struggled to maintain elaborate rituals when offerings grew scarce. Marble pillars in old temples cracked, unrepaired for decades.

This decay exacerbated social tensions. The gulf between a small elite (willing to collaborate with foreign governors) and the impoverished majority widened. In some towns, vigilante groups formed, attacking wealthy estates. Temple archives mention stolen grain from storehouses, and local scribes note that even temple property was no longer safe. Every famine or epidemic was seen as a sign of the gods' wrath. People whispered that the land was cursed, saturated with the **blood** of conquests and the tears of orphans. Hopelessness turned many to new cultic movements promising deliverance—if they performed the right secret rites.

15.12 The Final Persian Conquest and More Bloodshed

A brief moment of freedom came when native rulers like Amyrtaeus or Nectanebo managed to push back the Persians. Yet, these triumphs often ended in renewed invasions. The final Persian reconquest (under Artaxerxes III, around 343 BCE) brought even worse devastation. Memphis was said to have been stormed with brutal force; widespread looting left the city's temples in ruin. Some Egyptian accounts speak of mounds of skulls piled outside city walls, a monstrous reminder of Persian "victory."

Artaxerxes carried away more sacred statues, including precious images of deities from the old capital Thebes. Priests recorded these losses with sorrow and fear, uncertain if their gods could hear prayers without their physical images. The Persians installed puppet governors, punishing all suspected rebels. Additional fortresses sprang up across the Nile Valley, manned by foreign soldiers. For Egyptians living through it, each day threatened new horrors. Some pinned their last hopes on oracles that spoke of a distant "deliverer" from the west or north who would end Persian rule for good.

15.13 Dark Omens and Apocalyptic Beliefs

Living under constant invasion, Egyptians developed a heightened sensitivity to **omens**. A solar eclipse might provoke mass panic, with crowds weeping in temple courtyards, convinced the end of the world had come. A bizarre birth—like a calf with two heads—could be interpreted as a sign that the gods were punishing the land. Some priests capitalized on these fears, performing elaborate exorcisms or preaching that only hefty donations to the temple could avert doom.

It wasn't unusual for entire villages to gather at shrines, chanting spells day and night, hoping to ward off the next foreign army or plague. Some texts from the Late Period reflect an almost **apocalyptic** tone, describing cosmic battles between gods of light and darkness, paralleling the real battles that ravaged Egypt. People felt the boundary between the mortal realm and the chaotic underworld had grown thin. Tales of wandering ghosts, demon sightings, and cursed tombs multiplied, as if the entire land was unraveling at the seams.

15.14 The Arrival of Alexander and the End of an Era

In 332 BCE, **Alexander the Great** marched into Egypt, greeted by many as a liberator from Persian tyranny. Indeed, Persian forces withdrew without much fight. For Egyptians, this was yet another foreign conqueror, but at least Alexander showed respect to Amun's oracle at Siwa, presenting himself as a son of the god. Some Egyptians hoped this signaled a gentler rule. Temples welcomed Alexander if it meant the Persians were gone.

But Alexander's conquest also marked the **end of the Late Period** and the beginning of a new era—one dominated by Greek dynasties (the Ptolemies). For the Egyptians who had survived centuries of invasions and civil strife, the immediate sense of relief was tempered by the knowledge that foreign rulers still held the reins of power. Many wondered if the nightmares of the Late Period would truly vanish or if a new cycle of oppression loomed. The land had seen so much bloodshed and subjugation that fear had become an ingrained part of the national psyche.

CHAPTER 16

Magic and Sorcery: Realms of Fear in Ancient Egypt

Magic, or **heka** as the ancient Egyptians called it, was woven into every layer of their society. Farmers used simple spells to protect crops from pests. Priests performed elaborate rites to guard pharaohs in the afterlife. And in the shadows, cunning sorcerers allegedly sold curses to harm rivals. Though often seen as a pathway to healing or divine favor, magic also evoked **fear**—fear of unleashed curses, malevolent spirits, or unscrupulous magicians who might twist the forces of the unseen world for evil ends.

In this chapter, we explore Egypt's magical traditions from daily amulets to the darkest sorceries rumored to dwell in hidden scrolls. We will see how belief in cosmic power spurred both hope and dread among commoners. Tales of shape-shifting demons, undead guardians, and savage retaliatory curses highlight how magic was not just a tool for good but a potent weapon in the hands of those who invoked it. Ancient Egyptians lived in a constant push-pull: they revered magic as a gift from the gods while anxiously watching for those who might misuse it, bringing nightmares to life.

16.1 Heka: The Divine Essence of Magic

In Egyptian thought, **heka** was not mere illusion. It was a fundamental force created at the dawn of time, allowing gods and mortals to shape reality through words and ritual gestures. Scribes recorded spells on papyrus or temple walls, believing the correct recitation could heal the sick, banish evil entities, or ensure safe passage in the afterlife. Magic was so central that the creator god itself—variously Atum or Ptah—was said to have formed the world through spoken words, an act of cosmic heka.

Yet, if good magic built the cosmos, then the Egyptians also worried about "perverted heka," used to harm or kill. This belief introduced **mistrust**: your neighbor or coworker might secretly hold a scroll of curses to cripple your livestock. Skilled magicians were sought after but also viewed warily. People asked for healing amulets from them, yet feared angering them, lest they unleash a plague or demon in retaliation. The fine line between beneficial priestly magic and dark sorcery was never fully clear.

16.2 Protective Amulets and Fear of Cursed Objects

One of the most common expressions of Egyptian magic was the **amulet**—small charms worn or placed with the dead for protection. Shapes varied: the ankh for life, the djed pillar for stability, the Eye of Horus (Udjat) for healing and warding off evil. Most Egyptians, rich or poor, relied on at least one amulet. They believed these objects bristled with divine power to repel sickness, bites from venomous creatures, or wandering spirits.

However, the same amulets that protected could also be **manipulated**. A malevolent magician might craft a "reverse amulet," inscribed with twisted symbols meant to bring harm rather than protection. If slipped under someone's bed or hidden in their clothing, it could invite nightmares, disease, or accidents. Stories tell of families discovering cursed objects near their doorways—small clay figurines depicting them bound and blindfolded. Such horrific finds sparked terror. People burned incense, recited litanies, or hired stronger magicians to lift the curse. The ease with which an innocent charm could be corrupted fueled a climate where trust was fragile.

16.3 The Secret Recipes of the House of Life

In major temples, there existed a space known as the **House of Life**, essentially a scriptorium or library where priests transcribed sacred texts, including magical recipes. Access to these rooms was restricted. High priests and select scribes studied complex spells for healing the sick, protecting the king, or performing rituals that renewed the cosmic order. They also kept lists of "dangerous spells"—formulas that could kill, summon spirits, or inflict curses if used irresponsibly.

Ordinary Egyptians rarely saw these secret volumes, but rumors abounded: scrolls that could animate statues to do your bidding, or potions that turned a person's blood into scorpions. Some whispered that certain priests, lusting for power, memorized these dark spells. If they left the temple or felt slighted by superiors, they could use the House of Life's secrets against the unsuspecting populace. The thought that an aggrieved priest might conjure unstoppable plagues or monstrous apparitions cast a looming shadow over the temple's revered status.

16.4 Sorcery in the Courts: Legal Punishments and Fear of Accusation

Egyptian law codes, though not fully preserved, reflect that **sorcery** was a serious crime. Trials of alleged magicians occasionally appear in surviving papyri. Some defendants were accused of cursing high officials or attempting to manipulate the outcome of royal decrees. Punishments ranged from flogging and forced labor to death by impalement, depending on the severity of the offense. But proving magical wrongdoing was tricky. Did the accused truly cast a curse, or was it coincidence?

This legal ambiguity created an environment ripe for false accusations. If someone envied a neighbor's prosperity or suspected them of wrongdoing, they could claim that neighbor cast an evil spell. Officials might storm the suspect's home, searching for suspicious figurines or scrolls. Merely owning advanced medical texts or unusual incantations could be misconstrued as evidence of malignant sorcery. Fear of being labeled a sorcerer led some to destroy or hide any unusual texts, limiting the spread of medical knowledge and feeding a cycle of ignorance and superstition.

16.5 Funerary Magic: Spells to Ward Off the Dread Beyond

Death was the ultimate frontier where Egyptian magic shone. **Funerary texts** like the Book of the Dead or the Coffin Texts provided spells to navigate the underworld's perils—venomous snakes, fire-spitting serpents, demon guardians.

Mourners commissioned priests to recite these spells or paint them on coffins, ensuring the deceased's safe passage to the Hall of Judgment. Yet, the very existence of these terrifying passages—depicting lakes of fire, monstrous devourers waiting for unworthy souls—spooked the living.

Every Egyptian knew that without the right spells, a soul risked torment or oblivion. The fear was so strong that some families spent fortunes on funerary papyri. Rivalries formed when scribes offered exclusive "secret" chapters that guaranteed victory over the underworld's beasts. But if a scribe harbored ill will, might they subtly alter a single hieroglyph, dooming the deceased to eternal darkness? The possibility haunted wealthy patrons, reminding them how fragile salvation was in a land where magical knowledge held so much sway.

16.6 Love Potions, Enchantment, and Obsession

Not all magic was geared toward cosmic threats or lethal curses. Egyptians also used love spells and **enchantment potions** to sway the affections of a desired partner. Clay dolls or wax figurines might be inscribed with the target's name, accompanied by incantations beseeching deities like Hathor or Isis to inflame the person's heart. Some spells promised immediate passion; others threatened the target with madness unless they complied.

Yet, manipulating free will was deeply unsettling. Recipients who discovered they had been bewitched felt violated. Neighbors gossiped about individuals who acted strangely—"His eyes look distant, as if bound by a sorceress's cord." Accusations of love magic sometimes resulted in violent confrontations. Rival lovers might hire stronger magicians to break the enchantment or place a counter-curse, turning an innocent romance into a chain of retaliatory spells. Fear of hidden potions at taverns or secret incantations slipped into someone's food fueled distrust in close-knit communities.

16.7 Animal Magic: Totems, Familiars, and Terrifying Transformations

Egyptians revered many animals as sacred—cats linked to Bastet, crocodiles to Sobek, ibises to Thoth. Temple precincts kept these creatures under priestly care. Some magicians believed they could channel an animal's spirit to gain specialized powers: the keen sight of a falcon, the venom of a cobra. Folk tales spoke of shape-shifters who became wolves or giant cats at night to carry out mischief or revenge, though official texts rarely confirm such practices.

Regardless, the idea of an **animal familiar** or totem stoked fears that any stray beast might be a magician's eyes. Farmers in remote areas reported sightings of "demon baboons" dancing under moonlight, supposedly conjured by a reclusive sorcerer. Children were warned not to wander after dusk, lest they encounter a crocodile that was actually a vengeful neighbor. While many Egyptians dismissed these stories as fantasy, enough believed them to keep nightly curfews and rely on protective amulets—just in case.

16.8 Oracle Consultations: Blessing or Hidden Threat

Temples often featured **oracles**, where statues of gods "spoke" through hidden mechanisms manipulated by priests, or through ritual movements interpreted as divine signals. Egyptians consulted these oracles for solutions to personal problems—finding lost items, diagnosing illness, or identifying thieves. A "yes" or "no" from the statue could transform a peasant's fate. But oracles also carried a darker edge: a single divine verdict could condemn someone as a sorcerer or traitor.

If an oracle named you guilty, few dared question it, believing the god's voice was absolute. Families might disown relatives branded by the oracle. Some scribes hinted that powerful priests manipulated oracles for personal vendettas. Fear of being falsely condemned by a "rigged" oracle was pervasive. Yet people kept seeking oracles, desperate for divine guidance in a dangerous world. This paradox—needing the gods' word yet dreading a possible condemnation—reflected the ambivalent nature of religious magic.

16.9 Royal Magicians and Their Perilous Standing

Pharaohs relied on **royal magicians** to perform protective rites, interpret omens, and craft spells guaranteeing success in warfare. These magicians held privileged positions at court, but their closeness to power was risky. If a battle was lost or a plague swept the land, the pharaoh might blame incompetent or disloyal magicians. Legends describe sorcerers executed for failing to prevent catastrophes. Some accounts claim Rameses II or Seti I commanded magicians to conjure illusions to terrorize enemy envoys.

But high-stakes sorcery could backfire. A rumor that the king's magician had glimpsed the pharaoh's vulnerable fate could spark a purge. The monarchy demanded unwavering loyalty, and any sign of hidden knowledge about the king's potential downfall was grounds for suspicion. Thus, the royal magician lived in an environment where a single misstep—a flawed incantation or an unlucky omen—could seal their doom. Their mastery of spells offered security one day, only to be overshadowed by the threat of royal wrath the next.

16.10 Nightmare Tales: Undead Guardians and Haunting Spirits

Egyptian tomb art and funerary texts frequently depicted **undead guardians**—spirit creatures or reanimated corpses set to protect a burial site. Some magicians claimed the ability to bind a person's soul after death, forcing it to serve as an eternal guard dog. Or they might embed a curse that turned the mummy itself into a restless avenger. Whether these stories were literal or symbolic, they made tomb robbery a spine-chilling prospect.

Whispers of vengeful mummies roamed the Theban necropolis, with nighttime watchers reporting faint moaning from sealed chambers. People told each other about a craftsman who broke into a tomb for gold, only to find a withered hand clawing at his ankle. Even if these were exaggerations, they reinforced how deep the fear of magic-infused remains ran. The possibility of a half-dead guardian fueled superstitions that these tombs, already loaded with curses, were best left untouched.

16.11 Protective Ceremonies and the Cost of Safety

In times of crisis—plagues, invasions, or famine—entire communities might request **protective ceremonies** led by high-ranking priests or magicians. These gatherings involved chanting, incense, and sacrifices, attempting to banish evil forces. Skilled practitioners drew ritual circles or placed boundary stelas around the village. Some ceremonies lasted all night, with participants wearing masks to represent benevolent deities.

However, such ceremonies came at a steep price: temple fees in grain, livestock, or precious metals. For impoverished villagers, paying these fees could be ruinous. Those who could not afford it might be shunned, their homes excluded from the magical protections. Worse, if the ceremony failed—if the plague continued or an enemy army still arrived—frustrated townsfolk might blame the magicians for incompetence or hidden betrayal. Fear and desperation intermingled, creating a volatile situation where scapegoating was common. A single rumor of "the priest took our money but never completed the incantations" could spark violence against the supposed charlatan.

16.12 The Foreign View: Greeks and Romans on Egyptian Sorcery

By the Late Period and into the Ptolemaic era, **Greek** and later **Roman** visitors arrived in Egypt, fascinated by its magical reputation. Some Greek texts describe Egyptian priests as masters of arcane arts, capable of controlling elements or communing with gods face-to-face. These accounts, while sensational, confirmed the outside world's perception of Egypt as a land steeped in mysterious powers.

Yet, such fame could be dangerous. Conquerors might fear that Egyptian sorcerers could thwart their rule. Greek or Roman authorities sometimes banned certain rites, labeling them seditious. Magicians who offered to conjure illusions for foreigners risked condemnation from local priests who deemed them sellouts. The interplay of foreign curiosity and local suspicion further fueled anxiety around magic. Egyptians found themselves balancing a legacy of spiritual power with the dread that outsiders might exploit or suppress their traditions.

16.13 Late Adaptations: Coptic and Hermetic Influences

Even after Alexander's conquest and into the later centuries (moving toward the Roman period), Egyptian magic evolved. Some texts show a blend of **Coptic language** (early Egyptian Christian dialect) with older spells, indicating an ongoing tradition of local sorcery layered with new religious elements. Hermetic writings, attributed to the legendary Hermes Trismegistus, mixed Greek philosophy with Egyptian lore, discussing alchemy, astrology, and hidden cosmic truths.

Although these developments lay slightly beyond the pharaonic era, they continued the pattern: **magic as a double-edged sword**, offering secret knowledge but also inciting fear of misuse. Small cults might gather in desert shrines, performing rites under the stars, chanting half-forgotten hymns to Thoth or Isis. Town dwellers gossiped that these gatherings involved blood sacrifices or necromantic spells. The Egyptian government, now often in foreign hands, was either indifferent or punitive, adding to the cloak of secrecy. People still yearned for heka to shield them from a hostile world, but the risk of condemnation remained high.

CHAPTER 17

Demons, Spirits, and the Afterlife's Monsters

Ancient Egypt is often associated with grand temples, elaborate funeral rites, and a pantheon of gods like Ra, Osiris, and Isis. But behind these familiar deities lurked **lesser-known entities**—demons, chaotic spirits, and bizarre creatures said to inhabit both the mortal realm and the afterlife. Egyptians did not necessarily see these beings as wholly evil; many functioned as guardians or neutral forces. Yet, the fear they inspired was genuine. From shape-shifting spirits prowling desert roads to monstrous demons devouring those found unworthy in the Underworld, these supernatural forces added a darker dimension to Egyptian religious life. In this chapter, we delve into the **shadows** of Egyptian cosmology, exploring the realm of demons, wandering spirits, and the monstrous trials that awaited souls after death.

17.1 Defining Demons in Egyptian Thought

In modern usage, "demon" often implies a malevolent entity. However, **Egyptian demons** (sometimes called *daemons* in scholarly works) occupied a more complex space. They could be helpers, messengers, or dangerous obstacles depending on context. Many had composite forms—human bodies with animal heads, or vice versa—and names that evoked violent imagery.

- **Malevolent Spirits vs. Neutral Guardians:** Some demons were purely malicious, said to cause disease or misfortune. Others acted as gatekeepers or envoys of gods, testing or punishing humans who broke taboos.
- **Multiplicity of Purpose:** A single demon might cure illness in one circumstance and inflict suffering in another. The lines between helpful and harmful were blurred, fostering constant **caution** among Egyptians.

This ambiguity fueled **fear**: if you encountered a demon, how did you know whether it intended to guide or destroy you? Only specialized priests or magicians might interpret its purpose through incantations. A wrong guess could lead to disaster.

17.2 The Role of Demons in Daily Life

Demons were not confined to tombs or temples. Egyptians believed these spirits could **wander** the living world, lurking near marshes, deserts, or even busy cities. Folklore abounded with cautionary tales:

1. **Household Plagues:** If a family angered a local deity or neglected offerings, a demon might slip into the home, causing nightmares, food spoilage, or sudden illness.
2. **Desert Dangers:** Caravans crossing remote sands told stories of shadowy figures that led travelers astray, vanishing into dust storms. Some called them "desert demons," believed to be restless spirits of bandits or lost nomads.
3. **Night Terrors in the Streets:** In Thebes or Memphis, nighttime travelers sometimes claimed to see flickers of light or hear eerie cries—signs of demonic presence. Guards might shrug it off, blaming jackals or wild dogs, but rumor insisted that **wandering spirits** roamed city outskirts, hungry for unsuspecting souls.

Such tales reinforced an atmosphere where **commoners** lived with constant vigilance, performing small rites—like scattering protective incense or wearing amulets shaped like protective gods—to ward off unseen forces.

17.3 Desert Entities and Shape-Shifters

Egyptians had a special dread of the **desert**, often called the "Red Land," a domain of chaos beyond the fertile Nile banks. This region was linked to the god Set, known for disorder and storms. Many Egyptians also believed it crawled with spirits:

- **Desert Wanderers:** Legends spoke of mutated creatures, half-human and half-beast, cursed to roam dunes. Some might be the twisted remains of criminals exiled to the desert, now turned into **shape-shifting** spirits.
- **Animal-Headed Demons:** Jackal- or hyena-headed entities that traveled in packs, harassing lonely caravans. A lost traveler might see glowing eyes on a dune crest before vanishing into the night.

- **Phantom Oases:** Certain illusions enticed the thirsty to chase a mirage, only to vanish. Some said demons created these mirages to lure the living to their doom.

The desert's harsh conditions—the intense heat, sudden sandstorms—were themselves terrifying, but coupling them with rumors of malevolent spirits turned the **Red Land** into a realm of nightmares. Merchant caravans developed protective rituals, chanting spells at sunrise and sunset, trying to keep desert demons at bay.

17.4 Underworld Monsters: Guardians of the Afterlife

While daily life included demon sightings, the **Underworld** (Duat) held the most terrifying array of spirits and monsters. The Egyptian afterlife was no peaceful haven. Souls had to pass through a labyrinth of gates, each guarded by formidable beings. Spell collections like the **Book of the Dead** or the **Amduat** depict a vast bestiary:

1. **Serpents Breathing Fire:** Called "the Flaming One," some serpents coiled around a lake of fire, prepared to strike trespassing souls.
2. **Lions with Blazing Manes:** Positioned at gates to pounce on the unworthy.
3. **Axe-Wielding Demons:** Often shown as humanoid forms with knives for hands or axes replacing arms.
4. **Headless Guardians:** A class of demon that roamed the corridors of the underworld carrying their own heads, a horrifying spectacle meant to terrify the unsuspecting spirit.

Souls who lacked proper spells or amulets were easy prey for these watchers. The Egyptians learned from tomb texts that only the correct "password" or offering could calm each demon. This spurred families to invest heavily in funerary scrolls, lest their loved ones become fodder for underworld monsters.

17.5 The Weighing of the Heart: Fear of Ammut

One of the most iconic trials in the Egyptian afterlife was the **Weighing of the Heart** before Osiris. The heart was placed on a scale balanced against the feather of Maat (truth/justice). If it weighed too heavy with sin, the demoness **Ammut** devoured it, causing the soul's eternal extinction. Ammut herself was a horrifying composite:

- Crocodile jaws
- Lion's torso
- Hippopotamus hindquarters

To Egyptians, these three dangerous creatures fused into a single devourer. Ammut's role was crucial: she prevented the unworthy from advancing. But the terror of having one's heart eaten—ceasing to exist forever—loomed large in Egyptian spirituality. Some described Ammut as lurking near the scales with drooling jaws, eyes fixed on hearts that might tip the scale. This final "death of the soul" was dreaded even more than mortal death. People strove to live ethically and perform rituals ensuring a balanced heart, for fear of being **devoured** and erased.

17.6 Hierarchy of Spirits: From Minor Imps to Gatekeepers

Not all Egyptian demons ranked equally. Texts mention a virtual "hierarchy" of spirits:

1. **Minor Imps:** Low-level troublemakers causing small-scale mischief—souring milk, knocking objects over at night.
2. **Disease Bringers:** Specialized spirits or lesser deities carrying plagues or curses, often linked to scorpions, snakes, or nightmares.
3. **Gatekeepers or Heralds:** These more powerful beings served major gods, controlling who entered restricted sacred spaces or certain afterlife regions.
4. **High Demons or Cosmic Monsters:** Rarely encountered but devastating—like the serpent Apophis (Apep), the embodiment of chaos who nightly attacked the sun god Ra.

Egyptian tradition taught that each tier of demon required a **different** approach. Low-level spirits might be driven off by household charms. A Gatekeeper demanded elaborate incantations or priestly intervention. Apophis warranted cosmic-scale rituals, performed by priests at dawn and dusk to ensure the sun overcame darkness. This complex demonology underscored how well Egyptians systematized the world of spirits, yet also revealed their deep-seated **anxiety** that chaos lurked at every level of existence.

17.7 Apophis: The Eternal Enemy of the Sun

Among all the monstrous demons, **Apophis (Apep)** stood as the prime symbol of cosmic evil. Typically depicted as a colossal serpent, Apophis resided in the eternal darkness outside creation. Each night, as Ra journeyed through the underworld on his solar barque, Apophis attacked, trying to devour the sun or barge. If Apophis succeeded, the sun would fail to rise, plunging the world into endless darkness.

- **Daily Battleground:** Priests performed rituals at temples, reciting "spells against Apophis," hacking effigies of the serpent to aid Ra in this nocturnal battle.
- **Cosmic Dread:** Egyptians lived in **constant fear** that one night Apophis might win. Earthquakes, storms, or eclipses were interpreted as moments when Apophis gained the upper hand.
- **Iconic Image:** Some tomb paintings show Ra stabbing a giant coiled serpent, or gods binding Apophis with chains of fire. This demonstrates how central—and frightening—the threat of chaos was in Egyptian minds.

Despite the daily victory of Ra, Apophis was immortal. He could be subdued but not destroyed, ensuring **eternal conflict**. This cyclical drama fueled existential terror: the world balanced precariously between cosmic order and chaos, teetering on the outcome of a nightly confrontation with a monstrous serpent.

17.8 Exorcisms and Spirit-Banishment Rituals

Given the prevalence of spirits, Egyptians developed exorcism rites. Priests or magicians specialized in **spirit-banishing spells**, calling upon protective deities like Hathor, Sekhmet, or the primeval gods to drive out evil influences. A typical exorcism might involve:

1. **Incantations with Loud Recitation:** Invoking gods by name, threatening the spirit with divine punishment if it refused to depart.
2. **Use of Offerings or Lustrations:** Sacrificial incense, water poured over figurines to purify and "capture" the spirit.
3. **Dramatic Gestures:** Stabbing clay effigies representing the demon, spitting or trampling them underfoot.
4. **Amulet Placement:** Wrapping the victim in fresh linen while reciting protective formulas, sealing their body against re-entry by malicious spirits.

Failure in such a ritual could be catastrophic—priests themselves might be attacked by the enraged spirit, or the spirit might lash out at bystanders. Observers recounted "awful shrieks" or bizarre phenomena (sudden winds, flickering torches) as proof that real supernatural forces clashed during an exorcism. The entire village might gather to watch, simultaneously craving the ritual's success and fearing a partial failure that could unleash the demon on them.

17.9 Ghostly Apparitions and Restless Dead

Not all spirits were demonic by nature. **Ghosts** of deceased humans sometimes lingered if burial rites were incomplete or if the dead harbored grudges. Egyptians believed a **proper funeral** with prayers and offerings was essential to help a soul transition peacefully. If neglected, the spirit could become resentful, haunting relatives or neighbors. Typical ghost stories included:

- **Wailing Shades:** Heard near cemeteries at dusk, lamenting their abandoned tomb or lack of funerary offerings.

- **Revengeful Relatives:** Family members who died under suspicious circumstances might plague the living until justice was served.
- **Envious Ghosts:** The poor or outcast who, in death, saw that wealthier folk had lavish tombs, sought to disrupt the living in jealousy.

Egyptians answered these hauntings by leaving fresh offerings at neglected tombs, reciting **Letters to the Dead** to appease or negotiate with upset spirits. Some also hired magicians to forcibly banish a troublesome ghost. This interplay of guilt, fear, and ritual appeasement shaped how communities responded to any suggestion that "someone's spirit cannot rest."

17.10 The Liminal Zones: Temple Corridors and Tomb Entrances

Egyptians recognized **liminal zones**—thresholds between worlds—where spiritual energy was especially potent. Temple corridors leading to the Holy of Holies or tomb entrances were prime examples. Many sought blessings in these areas, but also dreaded them:

- **Temple Corridors at Night:** Priests might patrol them with lamps. Shadows cast by statues seemed to move. Some whispered that guardian demons roamed, punishing intruders or unfaithful priests.
- **Tomb Entrances after Dusk:** Workers seldom lingered near tomb doorways once the sun set. Even during construction, accidents or odd echoes in the corridors were blamed on ghosts or lurking gatekeepers.
- **Elaborate Warnings:** Painted warnings or small guardians carved in stone often adorned these thresholds, depicting gods with knives or monstrous watchers. The message was clear: "Beyond this point, spirits hold dominion."

Tales abounded of novices fainting upon glimpsing a flicker of otherworldly presence in a dim corridor, or faint growls heard behind sealed tomb doors. Whether real or imagined, these experiences fed the **collective fear** that crossing certain boundaries after dark risked an encounter with forces beyond mortal control.

17.11 Mythic Battles and Human Sacrifice Rumors

Though human sacrifice was not a mainstream Egyptian practice in most eras, rumors persisted that certain cults or renegade priests sacrificed captives to appease or bind powerful demons. Some extremist movements—possibly small or short-lived—were accused of staging **mythic re-enactments**: capturing victims representing cosmic enemies and slaughtering them at midnight to honor formidable spirits.

Such tales, if true or even partly believed, terrified the population. Parents warned children never to wander near isolated shrines or deserted temples at night. Soldiers posted near frontier forts claimed they occasionally found remains in remote chapels, hinting at dark rites. Officially, the state condemned these acts as heretical. Still, the **whispered possibility** that rogue priests might feed a demon with human blood cast a shadow over lesser-known cults and unregulated magical sects, fueling superstition and suspicion.

17.12 Influence of Foreign Demons: Late Period and Beyond

During the Late Period and subsequent foreign occupations (as we saw in Chapter 15), Egyptians encountered gods and demons from other cultures—Assyrian, Phoenician, Greek, or Persian. Some aspects merged with local beliefs, creating **hybrid demons** or adopting foreign monstrous figures into Egyptian lore. This cultural crossover could intensify fear:

- **Assyrian Night Fiends:** Soldiers returning from campaigns told of winged monsters from Mesopotamian myths, said to slip into Egyptian homes under new names.
- **Persian Devs and Daevas:** Zoroastrian concepts of demon-like devs might blend with Egyptian demonology, producing new terrors.
- **Greek Underworld Shades:** Greek settlers in the Delta brought their own ghost stories, sometimes synchronizing with Egyptian ghosts or chthonic beings.

People struggled to keep track of evolving pantheons, uncertain which ritual could banish a foreign demon. Some priests scrambled to incorporate these strange entities into known spells. Confusion gave these new spirits an **ominous aura**, as if unstoppable by traditional methods.

17.13 Demons as Instruments of Justice

Not all demon tales ended in tragedy. Some Egyptians believed that spirits enforced **cosmic justice**. Wrongdoers who escaped human law might be pursued by vengeful demons or ghostly avengers. A murderer who bribed officials could still face nightmares, injuries, or sudden death, attributed to an outraged spirit. In such narratives:

- **Revenge from Beyond:** The victim's ba (soul) or a dispatched demon overcame bribery or political power, balancing the scales.
- **God-Sent Chastisement:** Deities like Isis or Horus might unleash demon-servants to punish those who violated temple lands, robbed tombs, or harmed pregnant women.

This could comfort ordinary Egyptians, ensuring that **fear** of supernatural retribution replaced the failing human justice system. At the same time, it confirmed that nowhere was safe if the gods judged you guilty. Even fleeing the city would not hide you from an airborne demon or a restless ghost hounding your footsteps.

17.14 Surviving the Afterlife: Endless Vigilance

From childhood on, Egyptians learned that **life after death** involved a dangerous journey. They memorized spells, wore amulets, and funded funerary texts to navigate the demon-infested Duat. Families told cautionary bedtime stories:

> "If you do not recite Spell 125 properly, the serpent with a thousand knives will shred you before you see Osiris."

> "Disrespect your parents, and you will wander blind in the underworld, easy prey for hyena-headed devourers."

This conditioning made spiritual security a lifelong pursuit. Yet the cost could be burdensome: commissioning a Book of the Dead was expensive; amulets and priestly rites demanded constant offerings. The fear of **not being prepared** for demonic ambush in the afterlife overshadowed everyday budgeting decisions. Some peasants starved themselves to afford a single protective scroll for the family tomb, trusting it would guard them from monstrous judges beyond the grave.

17.15 Shifts in Later Centuries: Ptolemaic and Roman Period Syncretism

After Alexander's conquest and throughout the Ptolemaic and Roman rule, demonology evolved further. Greek or Roman gods syncretized with Egyptian deities, producing new forms. Some texts show elaborate **magical gems** carved with bizarre composite figures—part Greek, part Egyptian demons or protective spirits. Philosophical schools like Hermeticism added a layer of cosmic speculation, discussing spheres of archons or planetary demons.

While these new frameworks introduced a more intellectual perspective on the spirit world, the **fear** factor remained. Commoners still recounted nightmares about local demons, and tomb inscriptions continued to caution intruders with the threat of monstrous guardians. Even in more cosmopolitan cities like Alexandria, where Greek influences were strong, superstitious dread of hidden forces persisted. Secret magical cults, rumored to conjure old Egyptian demons, occasionally surfaced in back alleys or desert shrines, fueling official crackdowns.

CHAPTER 18

Grave Goods and Macabre Burial Practices

For Egyptians, **death** was not an end but a transition into another realm. Ensuring the deceased's safe passage required complex rituals, from embalming the body to stocking the tomb with everything needed in eternity. Some of these customs, to modern eyes, might seem **macabre**—removing organs, placing them in jars, burying figurines to serve the dead, and sometimes including items that hint at grimmer practices like human or animal sacrifice in earlier eras. In this chapter, we will explore the **uneasy** side of Egyptian funerary preparations: how corpses were handled, the chilling details of embalming, the unusual objects found in tombs, and the lingering dread of what might happen if these rituals were neglected or disrupted.

18.1 The Meaning of Grave Goods

From the earliest burials in Predynastic times to the grand tombs of New Kingdom pharaohs, Egyptians filled graves with personal possessions. The concept was straightforward: **you needed in death what you used in life**. Weapons, jewelry, cosmetics, clothing, and amulets accompanied the corpse. However, over centuries, these inclusions multiplied into elaborate sets:

- **Food and Drink:** Jars of beer, wine, bread, and meat.
- **Furniture:** Chairs, beds, chests—some intricately carved.
- **Servant Figurines (Shabtis or Ushabtis):** Magical statuettes to work for the deceased in the afterlife.
- **Magical Texts:** Papyrus scrolls containing spells or entire chapters of the Book of the Dead.

While these items might appear benign or even comforting, they also reflected a **paranoia** about the afterlife. Egyptians feared lacking a necessary tool or protection and thus being vulnerable to underworld dangers. This spurred tomb owners—especially the elite—to overprepare, sometimes to a grotesque extent.

18.2 Early Macabre Customs: Retainer Sacrifice?

In the Early Dynastic Period (c. 3100–2686 BCE), there is **archaeological evidence** suggesting possible human sacrifice at royal burials, particularly in Abydos. Rows of subsidiary graves around a king's tomb contained skeletons of young adults, some showing no sign of disease—raising suspicion they were killed or volunteered to serve the king in the next world.

- **Uncertain Practice:** Scholars debate whether these were forced sacrifices or attendants who chose to follow. Either way, the concept that human lives might be ended to accompany a ruler underscores the **fearsome** power pharaohs wielded.
- **Retainer Mummies:** Some tomb reliefs depict servants standing near the coffin, possibly symbolizing an entourage in death. Over time, real humans were replaced by figurines (ushabtis), perhaps reflecting a societal move away from literal sacrifice.
- **Lingering Shadows:** Even after this custom faded, rumors of sporadic "killings for the tomb" survived in folk memory, fueling a sense that some families might still face forced burial with a high official.

Though not commonplace in later eras, the memory of retainer sacrifice cast a **shadow** over funerary traditions, reminding Egyptians that the line between respectful burial and gruesome ritual could be thin.

18.3 The Grisly Process of Mummification

Mummification was central to Egyptian burial. Embalmers aimed to preserve the corpse so the **ka** (vital essence) and **ba** (individual personality) could reunite after death. But the process was **gruesome**:

1. **Extracting Organs:** Embalmers used hooks or small incisions to remove the brain and internal organs (liver, lungs, stomach, intestines). The brain might be discarded, while the other organs were stored in special canopic jars.
2. **Desiccation with Natron:** The body was packed and covered with natron salt for about 40 days, draining fluids and halting decay. Imagine a workshop where multiple corpses lay in varying stages of drying, the stench masked by resins and incense.

3. **Wrapping Ritual:** After washing and anointing with oils, embalmers wrapped the body in linen strips, often embedding **amulets** and reciting spells at each stage. Larger tombs required dozens or hundreds of yards of linen.
4. **Mask and Ornamentation:** Royal or noble mummies might have gold masks or elaborate cartonnage shells, sometimes with eerily lifelike faces. The sight of such a mask in a dimly lit embalming workshop could be unsettling—a rigid, golden visage staring back.

Apprentices in these workshops learned each step under strict secrecy. Mistakes risked the spirit's wrath or a reputation for sloppy embalming. Some believed that if an embalmer mishandled the corpse—dropping it, for instance—the deceased might haunt them. Indeed, the **fear** of retribution from improperly embalmed bodies lingered around the workshop, adding tension to an already macabre environment.

18.4 Organ Jars and the Protective Deities

The removed organs—liver, lungs, stomach, intestines—were placed in **canopic jars**, each guarded by one of the Four Sons of Horus: Imsety, Hapi, Duamutef, and Qebehsenuef. The jars' lids were shaped like human or animal heads. While these jars served a practical and ritual function, they also became **icons of dread**:

- **Strange Visages:** A jackal or baboon head on a jar could appear grotesque in dim torchlight.
- **Eerie Purpose:** Egyptians believed these deities protected the organs. But if the jars were disturbed, the guardians might unleash a curse or punish the tomb robber.
- **Spiritual Vitality:** Because organs were vital to resurrection, damaging them could doom the soul. This gave canopic jars a fearsome aura—vandalizing them spelled spiritual death for the deceased, and likely curses upon the vandal.

Even family members, while preparing a loved one's burial, might be uneasy handling these jars. The idea that one's father's or mother's organs lay sealed behind the fierce visage of a baboon-headed jar was enough to **unsettle** even the devout.

18.5 Wealthy Tombs Packed with Oddities

For the wealthy, tomb preparations escalated into vast collections of **luxury items** and **strange objects**:

- **Exotic Animals:** Some pharaohs or nobles included mummified animals—cats, baboons, crocodiles, even fish—believing these creatures might be companions or offerings to deities. In dark tomb recesses, row upon row of animal mummies formed a bizarre menagerie.
- **False Doors and Magic Portals:** Tomb builders carved "false doors" in walls, believed to be thresholds for the ka to move between the living and the afterlife. Approaching these carved doorways in flickering torchlight could give an uncanny sense that something might step out at any moment.
- **Miniature Servant Figurines:** As centuries passed, the use of shabtis (small figurines meant to perform labor for the dead in the afterlife) expanded. Some tombs contained hundreds or thousands. Stumbling upon piles of lifeless figurines, each with painted eyes, can feel like an **army of dolls** waiting to be awakened.

Archaeological evidence suggests these accumulations sometimes led to **logistical nightmares**. Embalmers and tomb workers, laboring late into the night to finish a near-limitless stock of items, found it unsettling that the dead seemingly demanded more goods than the living. Whispered jokes about the deceased's greed mingled with real fear that skipping any item might provoke a **posthumous curse**.

18.6 Grim Scenes from Tomb Art

Egyptian tomb walls, while often showing pleasant afterlife scenes, also contained **chilling vignettes**:

1. **Butchering Scenes for Food Offerings:** Detailed murals of cattle or fowl being slaughtered as funerary provisions. Knife-wielding butchers and bleeding animals were depicted with a matter-of-fact realism.
2. **Defeated Enemies Underfoot:** Some elite tombs boasted images of the tomb owner trampling or decapitating foreign captives, reflecting an

eternal dominance theme. The violence depicted—limbs severed, heads on stakes—could be disquieting to those unaccustomed.
3. **Underworld Trials:** Depictions of the deceased facing monstrous judges or crossing lakes of fire, suggesting a real possibility of torment.

For the living, the act of painting or observing these scenes was a reminder that **death** was fraught with potential horrors, from practical gore (animal butchery) to metaphysical punishment (underworld monstrosities).

18.7 Coffin Texts and Spells of Terror

Long before the Book of the Dead, **Coffin Texts** (emerging in the Middle Kingdom) were inscribed on wooden coffins. They offered a wealth of spells but also contained frightening references to **demons and traps** in the afterlife:

- **"Repel the Devourer"** spells: Detailed conjurations describing demon beasts with razor jaws. The occupant of the coffin needed precise words to prevent being eaten.
- **"Crossing the Fiery Rivers"** spells: Admonitions that scorching flames could consume unworthy souls.
- **Nightmare Imagery**: Some texts described bodily dismemberment or serpents lodging in a sinner's heart.

These spells, though protective, inadvertently fueled **fear**. Families reading or hearing them realized how perilous the path beyond death truly was. The coffin itself became a **literal library** of dire warnings. While intended to empower the deceased, it also underscored the dread of failing any test in the afterlife.

18.8 The Risks of Robbing the Dead

Tomb robbery was common, driven by the wealth buried with pharaohs and nobles. But it carried mortal and **supernatural** risks:

1. **Trapped Corridors and Hidden Shafts:** Some tombs boasted false floors that dropped intruders into pits. Workers claimed to find skeletons of robbers who'd starved at the bottom.

2. **Poison or "Cursed Air"**: Rumors abounded of toxic substances, mold, or putrid gases left to suffocate thieves. While not always intentional, the decaying materials could indeed be lethal in sealed chambers.
3. **Spells Against Trespassers**: Walls might include inscriptions warning of **divine wrath**. Even if these "curses" were symbolic, they preyed on thieves' minds. If misfortune befell a robber afterward—a fever or accident—it proved the tomb's curse was real.
4. **Mutilated Mummies as Warnings**: Some tomb owners allegedly displayed the remains of captured robbers near the entrance. True or myth, it fostered an intimidating aura that discouraged casual theft.

These factors turned grave robbing into a realm of real horror—knowing the tomb's occupant wanted to protect their valuables even in death, possibly with measures more terrifying than any living guard.

18.9 Animal Sacrifices and Mass Burials

Not all funerary sacrifices were human. Animal sacrifices, though more common, could also be disturbing:

- **Mass Animal Mummies**: Certain temples dedicated to animal cults—like the Serapeum at Saqqara for Apis bulls—accumulated thousands of mummified creatures. Corridors lined with bull mummies in massive stone sarcophagi gave a surreal impression of an **underground necropolis** of beasts.
- **Household Pets**: Some people chose to bury their pets with them, presumably to have companionship. In some instances, skeletal remains of dogs or cats were found in the tomb corridor, suggesting they might have been locked inside alive or euthanized to join the master. This raised **ethical discomfort** among certain classes who considered it a harsh practice.

Mass burials of ibis birds or crocodiles also point to large-scale ritual offerings that must have involved slaughtering countless animals at once. The grotesque scale—heaps of bones or leftover wrappings—reminded Egyptians that devotion to the gods could take **grim** forms.

18.10 The Tools of Embalmers: Hooks, Knives, and Dark Repute

Embalmers carried specialized tools, many of which looked ominous:

- **Brain Hooks:** Long metal or reed rods to pull brain tissue through the nasal cavity.
- **Cutting Knives:** Razor-sharp to slice open the abdomen.
- **Measuring Scoops:** Possibly for scooping out internal matter or applying resins.

While revered for their skill, embalmers were also **feared**. Handling corpses made them ritually impure in some eyes, and rumors persisted they might use leftover body parts for sinister rituals. Some believed they took an organ now and then for secret magical experiments or sold them to shady sorcerers. Whether such rumors were real or exaggerated, the hush around embalmers' workshops, with piles of used natron and jars of bodily fluids, contributed to their **unsettling** mystique.

18.11 The Cult of Osiris and Imitations of Death

Osiris, the lord of the underworld, stood at the heart of many funerary customs. Festivals like the **Mysteries of Osiris** included rituals reenacting his death and resurrection. Sometimes participants molded effigies of Osiris from mud or grain, "planting" them to symbolize rebirth. But certain phases of the festival reportedly involved:

- **Mock Coffin Processions:** Where a statue of Osiris was carried with great lamentation. Observers had to show genuine grief or risk offending the god.
- **Nighttime Vigils:** The effigy was said to "die" at dusk, only to be reborn at dawn. Meanwhile, the crowd chanted spells. In the flickering torchlight, the boundaries between the real dead and a symbolic representation blurred.
- **Whispers of Blood Rites:** Some localized cults might have included more intense ceremonies—blood from animal sacrifice poured on Osiris

effigies. The spectacle of dark-red fluid soaking a statue gave a potent, macabre charge to the event.

Ordinary villagers felt both awe and **apprehension** attending these rites, uncertain if they merely witnessed a pious drama or skirted the edges of dark magic. The omnipresent fear was: if Osiris's rites were mishandled, fertility might fail, or the next life could be jeopardized for the entire community.

18.12 Covert Burials and Secret Tombs

Over time, tomb robbery forced embalmers and tomb workers to bury kings and nobles in **secret locations**. Some pharaohs of the New Kingdom were moved to hidden caches like DB320 or KV35 in Thebes. The process of relocating mummies at night, accompanied by chanting priests, created an **eerie** atmosphere:

- **Nocturnal Processions:** Coffins carried by priests across moonlit desert paths, accompanied by muffled chanting. Villagers who glimpsed this from afar might see it as a funeral parade of ghosts or an act of grave violation.
- **Sealed Chambers in Remote Valleys:** Corpses stashed behind false walls, corridors caved in to hide them. The few who knew the secret risked being silenced or sworn to magical oaths.
- **Myths of Undead Guardians:** Stories grew that relocated mummies haunted the old tomb or roamed searching for their stolen coffin. The sense that these kings were forcibly "dislodged" from their eternal home added a **chilling** dimension to an already grim scenario.

18.13 Late Period Coffin Horrors

In the Late Period, as foreign occupations disrupted stable governance, funerary customs sometimes took on more extreme forms. Tombs might be smaller or constructed hastily, yet stuffed with near-ridiculous amounts of **protective bric-a-brac**: amulets, figurines, protective spells scratched on every surface.

Families were desperate to shield the dead from upheaval in both this world and the next.

- **Overflow of Shabtis:** Some tombs contained over a thousand figurines, crowding the chamber like a miniature legion, each holding tiny picks and hoes. The effect resembled a **mass of silent workers** waiting to be animated.
- **Recycled Coffins:** Economic hardship led some embalmers or families to repurpose older coffins, scraping off old names to inscribe new ones. If not done thoroughly, a tomb occupant might have mismatched spells. The resulting confusion could, in theory, cause a "fight" between spirits for ownership of the coffin.
- **Rumored Cannibal Hymns:** Recalling ancient Pyramid Text references to kings devouring gods for power, some Late Period cults allegedly revived these disturbing lines in secret rites, seeking to harness a fraction of pharaonic might. Whether true or exaggerated, it underscored the desperation of a society at constant risk of invasion.

18.14 Violations and Curses: A Never-Ending Cycle

No matter how carefully Egyptians prepared tombs—stuffing them with goods, writing curses on walls—**violations** inevitably happened. And each violation sparked new stories of curses. A single tomb infiltration might lead to:

1. **Public Outrage:** Citizens outraged that the sanctity of the dead was defiled. Some demanded vengeance.
2. **Supernatural Panic:** If the robber died soon after, neighbors claimed the tomb's occupant unleashed a lethal curse.
3. **More Protective Measures:** Surviving relatives then added additional curses, booby traps, or illusions in the next tomb construction.
4. **Continued Lore:** Tales of "evil eye" or "burning breath" guardians spread, further complicating funerary practices.

Thus, **fear** recycled itself: the more tombs were robbed, the more terrifying the curses became; the more terrifying the curses, the stronger the allure for bold thieves seeking rumored hidden gold. The cycle rarely ended, feeding an underlying sense of **macabre tension** across generations.

CHAPTER 19

Ancient Egyptian Medicine, Curses, and Superstitions

Medicine in Ancient Egypt was a curious blend of practical remedies, sophisticated knowledge, and deep-rooted superstition. On one hand, Egyptian healers demonstrated advanced techniques—setting bones, stitching wounds, and using herbal concoctions—far ahead of some contemporaries. On the other hand, fear of **supernatural forces** pervaded every aspect of healing. A cut might become infected not merely by germs (an unknown concept at the time) but, in their view, by an evil spirit or a curse cast by a jealous neighbor. This chapter delves into the **frightening** dimensions of Egyptian medicine: the intimidation of diseases personified as malevolent spirits, the ominous role of curses in everyday life, and the labyrinth of superstitions that dictated everything from diet to birthing practices.

19.1 Medicine as Battle Against Demons

Egyptian society viewed most illnesses not just as physical ailments but as **attacks** by malevolent spirits or the wrath of angered gods. This belief spawned a culture of **fear** surrounding sickness:

1. **Invisible Invasions:** If someone developed severe headaches or fevers, people explained it as a demon lurking in the bloodstream. Lacking the concept of microbes, they believed any body malfunction signaled either spiritual intrusion or divine punishment.
2. **Protective Amulets and Incantations:** Even while using herbs or bandages, physicians recommended wearing specialized amulets or reciting anti-demon spells. The goal was to **expel** the invisible attacker or appease the relevant god.
3. **Name Avoidance:** Just naming certain diseases gave them power, so some texts used euphemisms or shortened references, further intensifying the fear factor. If you mentioned a dreaded illness openly, you might "invite" it in.

Such an environment kept Egyptians on edge. A minor cough could escalate into panic if an oracle declared it was inflicted by an offended deity. Households rushed to placate the demon with offerings or hired priests to chant away the affliction.

19.2 Healers and Swnw: Revered Yet Feared

Healers, known as **swnw** (pronounced somewhat like "sun-u"), ranged from royal physicians serving the pharaoh to wandering village practitioners. Some possessed substantial anatomical and herbal knowledge, gleaned from **papyrus treatises** such as the Edwin Smith Papyrus or the Ebers Papyrus. Yet, despite their skill:

- **Alleged Curses:** If a patient died, families sometimes blamed the swnw for unleashing curses or lacking enough magical power. Fearing retribution, some healers demanded disclaimers or performed elaborate protective rites before treating severe cases.
- **Secret Knowledge in the House of Life:** Elite healers accessed the temple's House of Life, where advanced texts and powerful spells were archived. Gossip claimed these scribes might also learn "forbidden curses," able to afflict unsuspecting rivals.
- **Medical or Magical Quacks:** Alongside legitimate healers, unscrupulous charlatans offered short-lived cures. They peddled potions laced with unknown substances, or performed "extractions" of invisible spirits. When patients suffered complications, these quacks vanished, leaving behind stories of black magic gone awry.

This dual image—healer as savior but also potential sorcerer—cast a **shadow** over the entire medical profession, forcing conscientious swnw to conduct themselves carefully to avoid suspicion of practicing harmful witchcraft.

19.3 Herbs, Potions, and Fearful Ingredients

Egyptians used a wide variety of herbs and natural ingredients—such as **honey, garlic, willow bark** (containing salicin, a precursor to aspirin), and castor oil—for therapeutic purposes. But some concoctions appear frankly **unsettling**:

1. **Animal Organs or Blood:** Certain potions demanded parts of reptiles, birds, or even donkey blood for "vitality." Rumors of substituting human blood in extreme cures circulated, likely exaggerated but still terrifying.
2. **Excrement-Based Treatments:** Some prescriptions included crocodile or donkey dung as a remedy for burns or as a topical application. While partially tested for antibiotic effects, the smell and infection risk must have been high, leading to a fearful approach—only used if one truly believed in the supernatural potency of excrement.
3. **Body Fluids as Carriers of Magic:** Healers taught that bodily fluids—saliva, menstrual blood, or semen—could hold powerful magical energies. A few obscure spells recommended cunning uses of such fluids to banish or conjure spirits, intensifying the taboo fear around these materials.

Patients who visited a local swnw might witness these bizarre substances being prepared, hearing the physician chant dire warnings or specific curses to "activate" them. The borderline between genuine healing and **sorcerous** experimentation felt razor-thin.

19.4 Birthing, Midwives, and the Dread of Evil Babies

Childbirth in Ancient Egypt was fraught with **superstition**. Mothers faced real medical dangers—lack of sterile conditions, postpartum bleeding, infections—but also intangible threats. Midwives, who might double as wise women, performed rituals to ward off malicious spirits that allegedly targeted mothers and newborns:

- **Birth Wands and Protective Figures:** Ivory or wooden "birth wands" carved with protective deities like Taweret (hippopotamus goddess) or Bes (a dwarf-like god) were used to "draw a protective circle" around the mother. A single slip was believed to let a demon in.
- **Fear of Stillbirth or "Evil Infants":** Some believed a stillborn child could transform into a wandering spirit if not properly blessed. Rarely, whispers told of "demon children" born with deformities—immediately euthanized out of terror they housed an evil force.

- **Isolation and Taboo:** Mothers often secluded themselves for days, if not weeks, after delivery, avoiding contact with men or outsiders. The fear was that any negative gaze or curse from a stranger could curse the vulnerable mother-infant pair.

While these practices offered some emotional comfort, they underlined how **fear** overshadowed even the most joyous occasion. Midwives held precarious authority—revered for guiding birth, but swiftly blamed if a baby died or a mother developed fever, suspected of harboring incompetent or malicious magic.

19.5 Amulets, Curses, and the "Evil Eye"

Daily life in Egypt hinged on **warding off curses** from jealous neighbors or ill-wishers. The concept of the **"evil eye"** existed: an envious glare that could inflict harm or misfortune. Consequently, Egyptians wore amulets or painted protective symbols on walls:

1. **Eye of Horus (Udjat):** Believed to repel curses; ubiquitous in jewelry.
2. **Scarab Beetle:** Symbolizing rebirth, also used to block negative energies.
3. **Blood-Red Stones:** Some magical gems inscribed with protective spells, said to reflect the evil eye back to its sender.

Yet, ironically, the more people relied on these items, the more **paranoid** they became about potential curses. A dropped or broken amulet sparked immediate alarm: was it a sign the curse overcame their defense? Did they need a stronger remedy? This constant vigilance led to a thriving market for protective trinkets but also fed an undercurrent of fear that any casual glance or spat argument might escalate into a supernatural assault.

19.6 Maladies and Punitive Gods

In a land where gods were intimately involved in daily events, Egyptians attributed specific illnesses to specific deities or their retinues of spirits:

- **Sekhmet, the Lioness Goddess:** Associated with plagues. Her wrath manifested as epidemics. Priests recited **"appeasement texts"** daily to calm her. A sudden fever outbreak might prompt citywide prayers and sacrifices, fueling panic that Sekhmet was punishing moral lapses.
- **Hathor's Rage:** Linked to drunken festivals or love curses. People believed mishandling Hathor's joy (e.g., disrespecting sexual norms) could twist her gentle aspect into a punishing force.
- **Wadj-wer (Marsh Gods):** Bilharzia or waterborne diseases were ascribed to swampy deities. If neglected or insulted, they unleashed parasites causing bloody urine or extreme fatigue.

Communities undertook **mass rituals** to atone for collective sins or to calm the deity's anger. Drums, chanting, and incense processions might last nights, stoking a carnival of both hope and **terror**—hope for relief, terror that any misstep could worsen the gods' anger.

19.7 Menacing Medical Papyri: Spells and Threats

While some medical papyri were purely medicinal, others contained **ominous spells** that threatened malevolent forces. A typical papyrus might outline:

1. **Symptoms Explanation:** "If a man feels burning in his abdomen and sees nightmares…"
2. **Ritual Threat:** "I conjure you, demon of filth, by the Great Ennead, to depart or face the swords of Horus!"
3. **Practical Recipe:** "Grind thyme with honey; apply to the chest."
4. **Warning of Noncompliance:** "Should the demon remain, he will be cut into a thousand pieces by Sekhmet's claws."

These texts taught that healing was a **confrontation**—the swnw or magician threatened violent cosmic retribution to the afflicting spirit. A patient reading or hearing this incantation might shudder at the mental image of demons torn apart. Meanwhile, the physician, reciting it with grave seriousness, manipulated the patient's fear to strengthen the spell's psychological impact.

19.8 Methods of Diagnosing the Supernatural

To decide if an ailment was purely physical or curse-based, Egyptians used divinatory methods:

- **Incubation in Temples:** The patient slept overnight in a shrine, hoping the god (e.g., Imhotep or Serqet) would appear in a dream to reveal the cure or identify the curse. Some nightmares were so vivid that patients woke screaming, convinced they'd seen monstrous shapes.
- **Oracular Statues:** A small statue of a deity was asked yes/no questions. If the statue "nodded" after the question "Is a demon attacking this man?" the poor patient faced expensive exorcisms.
- **Observation of Animal Behavior:** If a cat hissed incessantly near the sick, or if a lizard scurried across them, it "confirmed" evil magic. That sign alone could drive families to blame a neighbor for sending the reptilian spirit.

Such interpretative techniques, blending scientific curiosity with mystical dread, occasionally spurred **witch hunts**. If the oracle indicted a suspected caster, punishment was harsh, ensuring entire neighborhoods lived in a swirl of anxieties about who might be cursing whom.

19.9 Life-Saving Surgeries and the Fright of Knife-Wielding Surgeons

Evidence shows Egyptian medics performed surgeries—trephining skulls, setting fractures with splints, and even minor incisions for abscess drainage. But imagine the **terror** of going under the knife in a world without anesthesia:

- **Binding Patients:** Attendants might forcibly restrain someone as the swnw made the incision, chanting protective spells to numb pain or keep evil spirits from entering the wound.
- **Blood as a Spiritual Vulnerability:** Bleeding was risky. Some believed that once blood left the body, it could be harnessed by malevolent sorcerers. Hence, immediate disposal or ritual burying of bloody bandages was required.

- **Operating Theaters?** Hardly. Procedures took place in corners of a workshop or near open courtyards, with watchers whispering prayers. The patient's screams and the smell of heated tools to cauterize wounds only deepened the **macabre** atmosphere.

Survivors sometimes credited the success to protective deities rather than the physician's skill, underscoring how deeply fear and piety underpinned every medical endeavor.

19.10 Malicious "Doctors": Cursing for Hire

Amid genuine healers, a shadowy class of "doctors" existed purely for **malevolent** ends. Some scrolls or local testimonies talk of individuals who specialized in producing curses or harmful potions:

- **Curse Vendors:** For a hefty fee, they would craft a wax figurine of one's enemy, stabbing it with needles or burying it in a graveyard to harness deathly energy.
- **Poison Masters:** Blending toxins from scorpion venom, snake venom, or deadly plants like hemlock. Victims died in agony, or succumbed to delirium, leading to rumors of demon possession.
- **Black Rituals:** These men or women might meet clients at night near deserted shrines. The flicker of torches, hushed chanting, and talk of summoning underworld spirits lent a deeply **sinister** air.

Though the state condemned such practices as crimes, enforcement was difficult. Fear of retribution by cursed "doctors" deterred many from testifying. Their existence spread a **chronic fear** that any feud or rivalry could escalate into lethal magic.

19.11 Love, Fertility, and Dangerous Charms

Egyptians valued love, fertility, and marriage, but these domains also brimmed with potential misuse of magic:

- **Fertility Rites:** Women seeking to conceive consumed potions laced with herbal aphrodisiacs. If unsuccessful, despair led some to suspect a hidden curse blocking conception, turning them to questionable magicians for more potent spells that might harm others inadvertently.
- **Love Spells Gone Wrong:** An obsession could brew if a spouse or lover turned away. Love charms sometimes morphed into malignant curses to enforce loyalty or cause madness in rivals. Families dreaded a scorned partner's vow: "I will see you cursed before the new moon!"
- **Birth Prognostication:** Checking the unborn baby's sex used onion bulbs or wheat seeds, accompanied by incantations. If results contradicted an oracle, panic ensued. Which "magic" was correct? Did a demon tamper with the test?

This blend of longing, heartbreak, and spiritual meddling made romance a **battleground** of curses and counter-curses, reinforcing that no aspect of life escaped the tension of supernatural fear.

19.12 The Legacy of Fearful Medicine and Curses

By the Late Period and beyond, Egyptian medical knowledge had spread to Greek and other cultures. Yet the hallmark of Egyptian healing remained the **fusion** of empiricism and dread:

- **Priest-Physicians:** Practiced advanced surgery but also relied on exorcisms and oracles.
- **Common Folk:** Stocked cupboards with protective amulets while suspecting neighbors of harboring ill will.
- **Royal Palaces:** Employed teams of swnw who simultaneously brewed healing potions and chanted anti-curse spells for the royal family.

In all these settings, fear was a **constant companion**—fear of disease as a spiritual invasion, fear of curses from jealous acquaintances, and fear that gods or demons might punish any misstep. While many Egyptians benefitted from the synergy of skillful remedies and magical confidence, the undercurrent of suspicion left them perpetually on guard. Even a moment of lowered vigilance could invite a hidden hex or malicious affliction.

CHAPTER 20

Decline of Ancient Egypt and Echoes of Fear

After thousands of years of relative autonomy, Ancient Egypt's political and cultural fabric gradually unraveled, culminating in foreign conquests that ended its long legacy as an independent power. This **decline** was neither sudden nor uniform, but a drawn-out process marked by internal schisms, decaying institutions, and successive waves of foreign rulers. In the midst of these upheavals, **fear** took on new shapes: fear of losing ancient traditions, fear of neglected gods withdrawing protection, and fear that foreign armies or new religious ideas would obliterate all that Egyptians cherished. In our final chapter, we examine how these anxieties surfaced in the **Late Period**, continued through the **Ptolemaic** reign, and lingered even under Roman control, shaping a civilization's final days and the haunting legacy it bequeathed to history.

20.1 Fragmented Kingdoms and Endless Intrigues

We have seen how the New Kingdom's collapse (c. 1070 BCE) birthed an era of **fractured rule**. Local warlords, priests, and city-based dynasties competed. The **Third Intermediate Period** (c. 1070–747 BCE) set the stage for centuries of instability:

- **Powerful Theban Priesthood:** At times, high priests of Amun held more real influence than nominal pharaohs, creating a "church-state" dynamic that stoked suspicion. Commoners wondered if priests served the gods or their own ambitions.
- **Army Factions:** Military leaders from Libyan mercenary backgrounds seized control in the Delta, establishing short-lived kingdoms. Soldiers often changed loyalties, fueling a **culture of betrayal**.
- **Constant Civil Strife:** Rebellion, local skirmishes, and blockades on trade routes. Families sought refuge behind walled enclaves, uncertain which warlord might appear at dawn. Hunger for stability grew acute, and every rumor of a new conqueror triggered mass panic.

Ordinary Egyptians, already living under the shadow of curses and tomb robberies, now faced daily threats from roving militias and unscrupulous local officials. The fear that a new overlord could forcibly conscript or enslave them became the **background** hum of life.

20.2 Nubians, Assyrians, and Persians: A Renewed Cycle of Terror

As discussed in Chapter 15, the **Nubian** and **Assyrian** conquests each left rivers of blood and looted temples. The Persians later repeated these patterns, imposing tributes and occasionally desecrating sacred sites. By the 5th century BCE:

1. **Temple Diminishment:** Many shrines lay partially ruined or pillaged. Priests lamented the "silence of oracles" as gods seemed absent. Fear of divine abandonment soared.
2. **Taxation and Forced Labor:** Foreign governors demanded heavy taxes, punishing late payments with floggings or worse. Egyptians dreaded the harsh Persian discipline that overshadowed daily life.
3. **Cultural Erosion:** Overlords introduced new customs or replaced local officials with foreigners, leaving Egyptians frightened their children would lose the old language and worship.

In these centuries, stories proliferated of **vengeful ghosts** of kings reappearing, lamenting the occupation, or cursing those who collaborated with invaders. While possibly legends, they expressed real anxieties about a homeland subjugated and gods unappeased.

20.3 The Ptolemaic Takeover: Greeks on the Nile

When **Alexander the Great** marched into Egypt in 332 BCE, some Egyptians welcomed him as a liberator from Persian rule. After Alexander's death, his general **Ptolemy** seized Egypt, founding the **Ptolemaic Dynasty** (305–30 BCE). On the surface, Ptolemies embraced local religion—building or restoring temples, fashioning themselves as pharaohs. Yet:

- **Greek Settlers:** Flooded in, receiving land grants and forming privileged enclaves. Egyptians felt overshadowed by Greek language and customs.
- **Hybrid Gods:** The Ptolemies promoted syncretic deities like **Serapis**, blending Greek and Egyptian elements. Many locals viewed this as an unnatural fusion, stirring fear that pure worship of Amun or Ra might vanish.
- **Economic Strain:** Greek aristocrats controlled trade and monopolized resources. Peasant farmers faced heavier taxes, reminiscent of earlier foreign regimes. Rebellions broke out in Upper Egypt, met with brutal crackdowns.

The old dread of foreign oppression mutated into fear of cultural extinction. Priests worried that if they cooperated too much with Greek rulers, the gods might punish them. Meanwhile, Greeks distrusted Egyptian magic, suspecting priests might invoke curses to sabotage the new order.

20.4 Rise of Apocalyptic Rumors

As centuries advanced, the sense that Egypt was irreversibly changing sparked **apocalyptic** visions:

1. **Prophetic Texts:** Late Egyptian or Demotic prophecies predicted a day when the Nile would run red or the sun fail to rise—a cosmic reflection of Egypt's despair.
2. **Temple Priests in Secret Conclaves:** Legend claimed certain priests met in hidden catacombs, chanting spells to resurrect old pharaohs who might drive out foreigners. The tension that these gatherings might incite another wave of brutal reprisals was constant.
3. **Oracles of Doom:** Some oracles, once a source of local justice, now issued dire pronouncements, suggesting the entire land was cursed until a "true pharaoh" arose. People shared these messages in whispered circles, fueling either hope or deeper anxiety.

Egyptians read each new plague of locusts, each unusually low flood, or each solar eclipse as a step toward the final **catastrophe**, confirming their civilization's downfall was near.

20.5 Cleopatra and the Final Dynastic Drama

The last strong figure of the Ptolemaic line was **Cleopatra VII** (reigned 51–30 BCE). She attempted to preserve Egypt's independence, forging alliances with Roman power-brokers Julius Caesar and Mark Antony. Egyptians witnessed:

- **Lavish Court Life:** Cleopatra's court displayed a blend of Greek and Egyptian traditions, fueling local gossip that the queen's flirtations with Roman generals might unleash yet another foreign wave.
- **Fear of Roman Legions:** Every rumor of Roman displeasure or Cleopatra's political missteps sparked panic that legions would arrive, pillaging towns as earlier conquerors had done.
- **Religious Anxiety:** Cleopatra styled herself as a living Isis, but internal skeptics worried that once Cleopatra was gone, the goddess's last champion in the palace might vanish too. Without Cleopatra's balancing act, the gods might truly forsake the land.

When Cleopatra and Antony lost to Octavian (future Emperor Augustus) at Actium (31 BCE) and later committed suicide, Egyptians braced for the worst. Indeed, in 30 BCE, Egypt became a Roman province. While many found peace under Rome's administrative structure, the sense of **doom**—that the last glimmer of pharaonic sovereignty had died—left a deep psychological scar.

20.6 Roman Rule: A New Fear and Cultural Decline

Under Rome, Egypt served as the empire's "breadbasket." The legions maintained order, and major temples like those at Dendera or Philae still functioned for a while. Nonetheless:

- **Heavy Exploitation:** Roman prefects taxed grain, controlling prices to feed Rome. Farmers risked severe punishment if harvests fell short. Tales of entire villages forcibly relocated or conscripted into labor.
- **Eroding Old Ways:** Over time, more Egyptians learned Greek or Latin for commerce, leaving old hieroglyphic scripts to an educated few. The sense that the ability to "read the gods' words" was vanishing frightened priests; many predicted divine wrath for ignoring sacred texts.

- **Magic Laws:** Roman authorities often viewed Egyptian magic suspiciously, banning certain rites. The "Isis cult" thrived abroad, but in Egypt, local temples sometimes faced restrictions. Practitioners who continued older, deeper arcane practices lived under fear of arrest or condemnation.

This tension wasn't always violent—Romans tolerated local faith to a degree—but Egyptians felt an **erosion** of authenticity. The grand festivals carried on, but fewer truly believed the old gods commanded affairs of state. Fear of a creeping emptiness in religious life gnawed at them, as though they performed rituals without cosmic meaning.

20.7 The Vanishing Priesthood and Threat of Heresy

As centuries passed, **priestly families** that once guarded millennia of sacred lore diminished. Temple lands were confiscated, endowments shrank, and fewer novices enrolled to memorize complex funeral liturgies or create the protective spells. Some outcomes:

1. **Temple Desertion:** Remote sanctuaries gradually fell into disuse, their corridors empty, statues covered in dust. Local peasants might scavenge building stones, intensifying the sense of a "godless" future.
2. **Survival of Underground Rites:** A handful of devout priests retreated to hidden chapels or continued performing the "old ways" in secret, rumored to offer specialized curses or oracles to the few who remembered them.
3. **Christians and Other New Faiths:** By the Roman era, new religions began gaining traction. Early Egyptian Christianity emerged, calling old gods "false" and old rituals "demonic." This shift provoked further fear among traditionalists that the final blow to Egyptian identity was at hand.

Some fiercely clung to the old pantheon, labeling Christian or other sectarian converts as "heretics" or "blasphemers." Scenes of temple vandalism, either by extremist new believers or by local opportunists, escalated tensions. Nighttime raids might smash idols or scrawl curses on temple walls. The gloom of watching beloved deities defiled spurred older Egyptians to cry out that the land was indeed losing the favor of all gods.

20.8 Tomb Looting on a Massive Scale

By the Roman period, a wave of **large-scale tomb looting** erupted:

- **Economic Desperation:** High taxes and diminishing farmland forced some peasants into grave robbery for quick wealth. They ransacked even the ancient royal necropolises.
- **Systematic Operations:** Gangs formed, systematically pillaging valuables from famed burial sites in Thebes or Memphis. Rumors implied corrupt officials turned a blind eye for a cut of the loot.
- **Desecration of Mummies:** In the rush for gold or precious amulets, mummies were torn apart, a sacrilege unimaginable in earlier times. Shreds of linen and bone littered the corridors that once gleamed with sacred spells. The living no longer feared curses as intensely, or they believed the gods had departed so thoroughly that no vengeance would follow.

For devout Egyptians, this was the final **horror**—the revered dead, centuries-old pharaohs or noble ancestors, reduced to shredded remains in the flicker of a thief's torch. The old curses and protective spells seemed impotent. Fear now turned to **fatalistic acceptance**: even the most majestic tomb or the mightiest pharaoh's name could not forestall the chaos unleashed by foreign occupation and internal moral collapse.

20.9 Lost Scripts and Diminishing Magic

Hieroglyphics remained the key to reading ancient religious texts. But under Ptolemaic and Roman dominion, usage of hieroglyphics shrank as **Demotic** (a cursive Egyptian script) and later Greek or Latin took precedence. By the 4th and 5th centuries CE:

1. **Temples Sealed:** Christian edicts or Roman policies closed many traditional sanctuaries, forcing priests to scatter or convert.
2. **Forgetting the Gods' Words:** Fewer scribes could interpret the old inscriptions accurately, leaving many magical texts locked behind an incomprehensible script.
3. **Legends of Hidden Scrolls:** People speculated about hidden caches of secret papyri containing unstoppable spells or curses, left unread because no living scribe understood them. The idea that unimaginably powerful magic lay dormant and lost behind forgotten glyphs fueled a new wave of **superstitious awe**.

As the language died out, so did the precise knowledge needed to maintain complex rituals. Some tried to preserve it through partial translations, but the deeper mysteries sank into oblivion. The fear among the last guardians was that once the words were entirely forgotten, the gods might vanish permanently—or become enraged by neglect.

20.10 Haunting Memories of a Great Past

As centuries rolled on, local Egyptians saw towering monuments from earlier ages—pyramids, colossal statues, deserted temple complexes—rising from the desert like **silent ghosts**. Most people no longer knew exactly which king built them or for which gods. The grandeur stood as a **testament** to lost power, but also as an eerie reminder:

- **Abandoned Monuments:** Stelae commemorating conquests or rituals, overgrown with sand, whispered of times when pharaohs commanded the known world. Now, foreigners ruled the Nile, mocking or ignoring these relics.
- **Stories of Curses:** The unstoppable curses once believed to guard these monuments apparently failed to repel invaders. Did that mean the gods departed? Or had the world changed so drastically that curses no longer functioned?
- **Tomb-Dwelling Nomads:** Some outcasts or impoverished families dwelled in tomb entrances, using them as shelters. They recounted ghostly apparitions or strange echoes at night, sustaining fear-laden folklore that the spirits of ancient kings still roamed, lamenting Egypt's downfall.

People lived among these ruins in **melancholy**: the sense that the greatest achievements of their ancestors had become lifeless husks, overshadowed by foreign doctrines and the unstoppable flow of time.

20.11 The Final Flickers of Pharaohs and Spiritual Resilience

Even after Cleopatra's death (30 BCE), sporadic revolts flared up, led by claimants invoking old pharaonic titles. Each attempt ended swiftly, crushed by Roman military might. Nonetheless, the common folk sometimes supported these rebels, hoping for a last restoration:

- **Brief "Pharaohs" in Rebellion:** Figures like "Domitianus" or others who minted coins with Egyptian motifs, claiming the gods chose them. But these ephemeral rulers vanished, leaving no mark but rumors of exotic rituals in desert strongholds.
- **Popular Belief in Oracle-Driven Miracles:** Some rebels brandished oracles from Amun or Sobek, promising a cosmic sign would drive Rome out. When no miracle materialized, cynicism grew, or fear that the gods had fully deserted them.
- **Maintenance of Folk Magic:** In rural districts, people quietly practiced the older rites—pouring libations, burying small effigies for harvest blessings—evading Roman suspicion. These folk traditions kept a faint spark of ancestral faith alive.

Despite repeated disappointments, a **resilient** spiritual core endured among many Egyptians. Even if formal temple cults waned, families clung to basic superstitions, lighting lamps for household gods, reciting fragments of ancient protective spells. Fear still bound them to the old ways, longing for a glimmer of the past's protective magic.

20.12 Epilogue: Echoes of Fear in a Transformed Land

By the 2nd or 3rd centuries CE, the classical age of Egypt was mostly overshadowed by the Roman Empire's broader concerns. Yet the **fears** that had shaped Egyptians for millennia did not vanish overnight:

1. **Lingering Tomb Curses:** Even Roman authors like Pliny wrote with awe or dread about Egyptian tomb magic. Soldiers posted near Thebes might avoid certain tomb corridors, mindful of local legends.
2. **Christianity's Rise:** As Christianity spread, it labeled many old rituals as "pagan demons." Some Egyptians who converted might have nightmares about being haunted by the old gods or by curses they once invoked.
3. **Mythic Memory:** Over generations, storytellers embroidered tales of unstoppable curses, fearsome goddess wrath, and vanishings among temple ruins. These legends formed a cultural undercurrent—vague recollections of how might and magic once coursed through the Nile Valley.

Eventually, the knowledge of hieroglyphics died out completely, sealing away the final secrets of the old religion. **Fear** thus persisted in ghost stories about half-forgotten gods or walled-up priests, rumored to still chant in hidden crypts. Unanswered questions about the fate of the gods fueled speculation that they might reawaken or that their curses still slumbered, waiting for an unlucky intruder.

20.13 Final Reflections: A Civilization Shaped by Fear

Throughout our journey—from prehistoric settlements to the last days under Roman dominion—fear served as a **powerful thread** binding Egyptian history:

- **Fear of the Nile's Wrath:** If floods failed, famine ensued, stoking terror of cosmic disfavor.
- **Fear of the Gods' Judgments:** Rulers used temple propaganda and tomb curses to maintain authority, weaving dread into the social fabric.
- **Fear of Curses in Medicine:** People balanced herbal remedies with exorcisms, suspecting demons lurked behind every ailment.

- **Fear of Foreign Conquest:** Invasions by Nubians, Assyrians, Persians, Greeks, and Romans fueled a perennial sense of vulnerability.
- **Fear of Lost Traditions:** As scripts vanished and temples closed, Egyptians worried about the gods' departure and the final extinguishing of the pharaonic soul.

In many ways, these layers of fear were also a source of **cohesion**: they spurred monument-building, fostered complex funerary rites, and sustained a shared identity in the face of chaos. Egyptians clung to rituals as bulwarks against a dangerous world, forging a unique civilization that left an indelible mark on history.

Conclusion

The **Decline of Ancient Egypt** was not a single collapse but a slow unravelling across centuries. Each new conqueror chipped away at the old order, each new crisis amplified the dread that had always simmered beneath the surface. The final absorption into the Roman Empire signaled the end of pharaonic sovereignty, but the echoes of fear—the fear that shaped medicine, religion, and politics—lingered long after the last temple closed.

Yet this is not a story of mere gloom. The Egyptians' response to fear spurred innovation in architecture, theology, and art. Their cosmic battles against demons, their protective tomb curses, and their elaborate funerary customs expressed a civilization's determination to transcend mortality and chaos. Even as foreign powers dominated the land, Egyptians preserved scraps of their identity through superstition, folk rites, and the abiding memory of the grand achievements of the past.

In the end, fear functioned both as a **weapon** (wielded by priests, pharaohs, and eventually foreign rulers) and as a **shield** (empowering individuals to seek protective spells, to place amulets on their children, to bury their loved ones with the means to outlast monstrous afterlife threats). The overarching lesson is that a culture's handling of fear can illuminate its deepest values and aspirations. Ancient Egypt's final chapters may have dimmed under Roman rule, but the resonance of its beliefs, curses, and supernatural dread survived in legends—still captivating the human imagination millennia later.

Help Us Share Your Thoughts!

Dear reader,

Thank you for spending your time with this book. We hope it brought you enjoyment and a few new ideas to think about. If there was anything that didn't work for you, or if you have suggestions on how we can improve, please let us know at **kontakt@skriuwer.com**. Your feedback means a lot to us and helps us make our books even better.

If you enjoyed this book, we would be very grateful if you left a review on the site where you purchased it. Your review not only helps other readers find our books, but also encourages us to keep creating more stories and materials that you'll love.

By choosing Skriuwer, you're also supporting **Frisian**—a minority language mainly spoken in the northern Netherlands. Although **Frisian** has a rich history, the number of speakers is shrinking, and it's at risk of dying out. Your purchase helps fund resources to preserve and promote this language, such as educational programs and learning tools. If you'd like to learn more about Frisian or even start learning it yourself, please visit **www.learnfrisian.com**.

Thank you for being part of our community. We look forward to sharing more books with you in the future.

Warm regards,
The Skriuwer Team

www.ingramcontent.com/pod-product-compliance
Lightning Source LLC
LaVergne TN
LVHW012105070526
838202LV00056B/5634